The Power of Peace
The Value of Meditation

Alternatives
Life Options for Today

The Power of Peace
The Value of Meditation

SHIRLEY WALLIS

Dedication: With Love and gratitude to
my Support Teams and to Brave Hearts everywhere.

First published in Great Britain in 1999 by
LONDON HOUSE
114 New Cavendish Street
London W1M 7FD

A catalogue record for this book is available
from the British Library

ISBN 1 902809 08 4

Edited and designed by DAG Publications Ltd, London.
Printed and bound by Biddles Limited,
Guildford, Surrey.

Contents

Acknowledgements

Thanks to my dear family and extended Soul family of friends, for support, wisdom and understanding. Thanks to Sandy Stevenson (author of The Awakener, Gateway Books, UK), whose wisdom, humour and practical approach is inspirational. All gratitude to Dr Norma Milanovich (USA) for bringing the Universal Laws and Metaphysical teachings into practical focus, through her dedication and service (co-author with Dr Shirley McCune, The Light Shall Set You Free, Athena Publishing. USA).

Introduction

What is creative meditation?

The primary purpose to this type of meditating is to promote relaxation in body and mind which will develop inner peace and freedom of spirit.

The experiences and benefits will slowly unfold as you sense and regain many latent abilities which build the structure leading to your own mind control. Regular meditation is the ultimate tool to bring harmony into your life, for like attracts like; and as you set out on this discovery you will find eventually that you are magnetising people, events and circumstances that match your development. Guidelines and hints for all ages, from the teenager to the more mature, are included in the following pages, whatever the belief system or cultural tradition. Creative meditation heightens your understanding of both your outer, daily life and your inner world through the focus and concentration that develop naturally as a result of giving yourself the time to explore. This personal input is an investment requiring 'set aside' time, starting with about five minutes, gradually increasing to nine and then, if you so choose, about fifteen to twenty minutes.

In everyday life, we are constantly by-passing the activities of the conscious mind which sometimes needs to digest and ponder, because we are trying to cram too much into too little time, thus producing stress. At the opposite end of the scale, boredom or dissatisfaction with life may take hold. We have got into the habit of creating diversions for ourselves by escaping into activities such as reading, watching television, movies and sport, socialising, drinking, dancing and often opting out altogether by going to sleep!

These are all physical ways outside ourselves of changing mundane routine, getting away from worries or diverting our attention. We generally call it our way of relaxing.

Using meditation as a tool to bring relaxation and well-being to all levels of your existence in a physical body may be regarded as having a secret asset – secret, because the experience is unique to you – you are in charge, with your own intent and self-motivation working in accordance with your needs.

There are many types of meditational disciplines – some are aligned to particular religious and cultural systems, but ultimately, they all encourage the participant towards finding inner serenity where a greater understanding unfolds. *Creative* meditation is a technique where you exercise your *imagination* with visualisation and sometimes sound, which develops and triggers your *intuition*. This process allows *inspiration* to flow actively into your thinking pattern as you meditate, and it is also increased as you go about your daily life.

Some may think that only a substitute, fantasy world is created through meditation – indeed, daydreaming has its place in life – but as the Power of Peace invades every cell of your body through meditating on a regular basis, a state of self-healing automatically and subtly occurs. For example, brain scanning and brainwave patterns have given us much information on the different levels or cycles of brain activity that take place when our minds shift from wakefulness into relaxation, sleep and deeper sleep. The 'alpha' state describes the state of true mental and physical relaxation that can be achieved through meditation, when chemicals called endorphins are released into the body to produce a state of harmony and well-being, while at the same time giving a boost to the immune system.

Nowadays, there are many medical practitioners and therapists who recommend the practice of meditation for many reasons, including heart problems, blood pressure and general stress.

We all have a different point of view as we look out and sense the world from our physical bodies. This base is a package of beliefs and experiences that we have observed as our 'truth' about ourselves and our view of the world and other people. Sometimes, that view becomes restricted with prejudices or assumptions which at some stage will form a barrier when a new challenge arrives to test our rigidity.

New, incoming data and discoveries in our personal lives may indicate that we *have* to change or be willing to develop our own, personal evolution as the world around us also constantly re-structures itself.

Many people feel threatened by change as if something outside themselves – which some call Fate – were taking the upper hand, making them feel helpless. Perhaps everything seems to be moving too fast and it becomes harder and harder to 'keep up'. Setting aside a little time for meditation will give you space – a few minutes in a relaxed state is of immense value – and when you find the deeper level of tranquillity, you will want to return again and again. Whatever your need, there is value in meditation for you, whether you start right away on your own, get together with friends or seek a teacher to motivate your intent. If you already meditate, then I hope you will try out some of the visualisations. Now and then, there may be a little repetition of some points which are just meant to emphasise their meanings, or they may link in to slightly different contexts, so I trust you will bear with me.

I have also referred to a number of 'alternative' subjects and ideas with which you may or may not be familiar. They are not explored in depth, since this book is designed merely to link with them in order to show how these, and for that matter, *all* subjects contribute to meditational practice.

Here, then, is an opportunity to tune in to yourself and the Cosmos and create a position of understanding as to who you really are and the nature of your destiny, with a practical approach and a positive structure for realising the value of meditation to find the Power of Peace.

Part One
PREPARATION GUIDELINES

1

The value of right intent, right time and right place

Meditation is the door to your own adventure. No one else can open it for you, but come ... come to the threshold ...

'What do I want?' and 'What do I gain?' are the types of question on our minds as we are attracted to the intention of exploring the Power of Peace through meditation. To have 'right' intent from the outset is desirable, for it is more than simply a matter of good intention; there is a measure of sincerity more than idle curiosity to this quest which involves doing the best for oneself, wishing to know how to do it, and perhaps, in the background, the longing for peace and freedom of spirit.

What you want out of life right now will largely depend on your age. Younger people dream inwardly of what they think they want and outwardly are guided by parents, guardians and teachers who show them how to fit into society, find their role and urge them to study and ultimately get qualifications for a job or career. Other interests such as sport, dancing, reading or even a part-time job have their place in the timetable.

Within this set-up of family and education, the body is also growing and maturing. There is such a lot going on! Confusion constantly pervades this game plan. If the teenager or student chooses to promote his or her well-being by giving the body and mind a few minutes meditation daily, it allows some peace and space in which everything has a chance to be re-energised and harmonise. Meditation works at a very beneficial, subtle level which aids concentration for any personality, whether a physically energetic or a quieter type. In Chapter 11 there are safe, special meditation guidelines and suggestions for the younger age group.

If you are not so young, you may feel dissatisfied with life in some way. *If only* ... you could change certain things, you just *know* you'd be happier. Usually the answer in this equation is money – unless you, or someone dear to you becomes ill or handicapped. The choice might then be health instead of financial wealth. (The older generation usually place a higher priority on this, for obvious reasons.) For some people, happiness may depend totally on others.

Thus health, wealth and happiness seem very important to our lives. *If you were to be granted just one of these as the wish for your lifetime, which would it be?* Think very carefully. Indeed, is there a *right* answer? Certainly, your answer will give you a clue as to where your 'values system' is coming from at the moment, and that will be influenced by age and present circumstances – or will it? What you choose may be right for you at this present time. So, after careful thought, choose either health, wealth or happiness and write it down on the inside cover of this book with the date.

Once you have read these first chapters on preparation guidelines and have started this course of meditation, we will pose this question again in the last chapter. There is no catch and you can't go wrong.

What do I gain? Our general motivation in life is influenced by the priorities and values which are applicable at the time and these are subject to the influences of the current trends, fashions and general publicity being generated on the mass consciousness level.

Behind this is each individual's ambition, their application to it and the sum total of their self-assessment so far. 'What's in this for me?' is the common question. But as regards our subject of meditation, let's turn that question around and say, 'What's in *me* for this?'

You are a collection of beliefs, thoughts, attitudes and emotions – a steady accumulation – which are stored into your databanks through your experiences in life. In short, there has been a programming going on since birth – and before that – through your genetic inheritance. Nor is it just the collection of genes determining your physical data. There are many invisible energy factors at play in the *whole* construct of your body, mind and spirit which you bring in total to the process of meditation, for they cannot be separated.

We shall examine this whole human package or, as I like to call it – *the third- dimensional (3D) spacesuit* – in Chapter 2.

Let's try an experiment. Wherever you are reading this now, whether in bed, on a train, in an armchair or relaxing somewhere, read the following, then close your eyes and do it. (Anyone around you will assume you have gone to sleep and won't take any notice. Only you and I know that we have a hidden agenda – the Power of Peace). It will take only a few minutes. Read slowly and don't nod off … just yet …

Exercise 1: Breath of Peace

Place your hands on your thighs and uncross your legs or feet. Close your eyes. You are feeling comfortable, relaxed, but not yet ready for sleep.

Focus on your breathing ... listen to your breathing. Breathe in and out only through your nose – not your mouth ... feeling more and more relaxed ... relaxing into the breath ... feeling quite safe with the Power of Peace enfolding you and protecting you.

Keep listening to your breath ... breathing in ... breathing out. If one of your airways seems a little blocked, concentrate a few breaths through that nostril by directing your attention to it. Keep your mind on that task ... breathing in ... breathing out. Don't force the breathing ... just focus upon it ... gradually clearing ... more and more clear ...

Now back to breathing slowly and with relaxed rhythm ... more and more relaxed ... *don't go to sleep* ... listen to your breath ...

Breathe in peace ... breathe out *STRESS*...

Breathe in peace ... breathe out stress ...

Breathe in peace ... breathe out stress ...

Now breathe in peace ... and breathe out peace ...

Breathe in peace ... breathe out peace ...

Breathe in peace ... breathe out peace ...

All is well ... all is at peace ... all is in harmony ...

May the Power of Peace be with you ...

Now take a *deep* breath and open your eyes. Blink them two or three times. Well done you. Easy, wasn't it?

It's a good idea now to eat a little something or take a drink, although the exercise took only a few minutes This will bring your energies back into the physical body or, as it is termed, *ground* yourself if you went into focus rather deeply. If you are in bed now or relaxing in a horizontal position, then you may feel ready for some sleep, in which case you won't need to ground yourself, for in the act of going to sleep, everything closes down anyway.

This Breath of Peace exercise, exactly as written, is an introduction to meditation and acts as a warming-up exercise of great simplicity, yet incorporates many hidden benefits. (Meditation 'proper' should always be done seated with the spine straight, as you will see later on.)

Just remember, to get to sleep at night, to de-stress yourself at work, school or when facing a challenge, take yourself off, sit down and breathe the Breath of Peace. As you do this, all those around you will benefit; or if you are alone, it will fill your surroundings with peaceful vibrations ... pets love it as well as humans!

The breath is the most important of tools for meditation. It is the creative link which generates everything else you do in the meditative state. Of course, in daily life, we are breathing quite naturally and take it for granted, but once breathing becomes stressed through a common cold or other dis-ease we become much more aware of it functioning. The voice, as sound – being behind the breath, is another powerful tool which interacts with your body, mind and spirit, as we shall see in Chapter 9.

Summary

To help you define your intent and motives, set out below are stages of development. Numbering them might imply that there is a sequence to be followed and that you have to accomplish one stage before you can go to another. The answer is both yes and no.

The meditation route is not a straight line of unfoldment, for the experiences are unique to each person. It is wise, however, to keep to the preparation guidelines so that everything becomes a very quick, routine. For example, we *always* do an initial relaxation routine and an opening and closing procedure for *every* meditation (see Chapter 4). After that, the development and benefits grow automatically over a period of time and progress only depends on how much dedication you are willing to invest in yourself and upon your chosen themes for personal development (e.g. breath relaxation, self-healing, spiritual guidance etc.).

Stage 1: Developing self awareness through Creative Meditation.

✳ Preparations (getting ready).

✳ Relaxation, protection (opening up).

✳ Breath and Breath of Peace exercises.

✳ Visualisation, focus and closing down procedures.

Stage 2: Developing a heightened, spiritual awareness through contact with Higher Self, (Angel Within) and Soul.

✳ Practice in co-ordinating self awareness with Higher Self/Soul and eventually other dimensional guardians (angelic) and teachers.

✳ Developing self-healing, ESP (Extra-Sensory-Perception abilities, e.g. telepathy).

✳ Channel Higher Self.
✳ Develop by seeking knowledge through study and the regular practice of meditation.
✳ Service/helping others.

Stage 3: Practice of conscious spiritual awareness.
✳ Natural development of multidimensional understanding of self.
✳ Becoming a seeker of Divine Knowledge. Further awareness develops a 'greater picture' to physical life.
✳ Soul awareness (fine tuning). Recognition of primary Soul Path or Soul Mission.
✳ Training and developing skills for helping others (service).

Stages 1 and 2 blend into each other very naturally once you get going. You can pick out specific meditations, simply do the different visualisations for exploring, or concentrate on finding the silence of peace. All of these you will find in the chapters devoted to Stages 2 and 3. It doesn't matter which you choose to do – all can give you many, differing benefits and learning situations.

Stage 3 is always unfolding in the unconscious background of life. From the moment you close your eyes in meditation or contemplation, it is naturally fuelled through the Power of Peace in the exercises of the first two stages. Of course, how far you wish to develop your spiritual nature further as a seeker for Divine Knowledge is up to you, and will unfold at the right time according to the Soul's direction. Once your sincere intent is to move in this direction, you will be attracting the right people, lessons and conditions to yourself in your own specific time frame as you become more and more in harmony with the Source.

Nothing can or should be *forced*. The basis of all meditation is relaxation and being in harmony. Remember, you are *not* ever involved in any competition and there are no hidden agendas or conditions attached. You are in charge and set your own standards for yourself.

Right time and right place
Having got through the barrier of whether or not to try meditation (or to try again), many people go through a 'yes but' situation. Yes, I'd like to do it, but ... I'll never be able to find the time ... I get home from work too late/too tired ... my family/partner/friends won't understand ... my children won't let me/they're too young ...

anyway, I'll feel daft ... and so it goes on. All genuine difficulties forming the second barrier.

Yes, of course this is something which needs to be fitted into daily routine in some way – but how?

Perhaps we need to know a bit more, to get some perspective. When is the right time to meditate? When can I find the time? How many times a week am I 'supposed' to meditate? And for how long?

Here, then, are some guidelines and suggestions.

* The right time to meditate is when it suits you.
* Finding the time has to suit your personal routine and lifestyle.
* The number of meditations a week can be one or two, or once or twice daily – again, it's up to you.
* The time you allow for each meditation can be from a minimum of nine minutes. A relaxation Breath of Peace exercise should take three to five minutes.

First of all take a good look at your weekly routine. Which day(s) might be suitable? If you live in a busy household, when are you totally on your own for ten to twenty minutes in any day? Answer: when you're in the toilet, bathroom, bedroom or study. Define the places in your living quarters that would be feasible to claim for your own for half an hour on a regular basis.

Bathrooms are overworked in the mornings and evenings but are usually empty the rest of the day. A bathroom can become your meditation room quite easily if there is nowhere else.

Getting your act together with thought and preparation motivates you into action. You are acting 'as if' all is going ahead and this action is sending commands to your subconscious that you are in control.

* Choose a chair which is always going to be your meditation chair (or stool).
* If you buy a second-hand one, you'll need to clean it up from the previous owner's vibes! As long as you can sit at ease with the spine straight and able to have both feet planted flat, on the ground, you've got the right type.
* Have cushions if you like – just be comfortable.
* Take your meditation chair to your chosen meditating space if necessary, or place it there permanently. Think of this area now as your personal sanctuary.
* You can make a meditating seat of your own. No one else should really use it. It could be in the form of a square 'box'

with a comfortable seat. This acts as a sacred space, as does a mat upon which you can place your chair (see picture).

* You can screen off the corner of a room/bedroom and keep it specifically for your meditations (if possible, this is ideal).

* Find a small table or suitable surface in front of your seat – a tray is useful – upon which you can place a lighted candle (and/or incense, flowers, crystals, as desired).

* Creating a peaceful atmosphere before you start reflects your intentions.

* Your sanctuary needs ideally to be away from possible impinging sounds which could be disturbing, like the telephone. Can you unplug it?

* If there are many people in your household, try to have a room where the door can be secured from the inside.

* The next important thing to do is to make a sign for the door! Keep it simple like 'Please do not disturb', and you could add ... 'Meditating'.

* Sometimes you will need a portable tape recorder to help you with visualisations. *Don't use a headset* as this will interfere with sensitivity in your ESP audio/visionary centres of the head.

* You need an electrical point for the tape recorder – or batteries.

* Be careful in the choice of a tape. At first, sounds of nature – birds and water are best – just gentle, non-intrusive sounds to give a peaceful background (see Chapter 9).

* Buy a new notebook to act as a journal in which to record (with the dates), your experiences. This could prove invaluable later on.

* Lastly, you may like to acquire a warm shawl, large scarf or poncho-type garment to use solely for meditation. Your body temperature drops a little when meditating, and keeping warm and comfortable, especially in winter, is a priority. Also, placing something special around the shoulders puts you in touch straight away with your intent.

Checklist

* Your own space.
* Your own comfortable seat to support the upright spine, enabling feet to be flat on the ground.

* Tape recorder (for electricity or batteries). *Not* a headset.
* Table or raised tray in front of you – at least a metre away from you – for a lighted candle, (incense, crystals, flowers etc. if desired).
* Meditating shawl/rug optional.
* Notebook/journal to record your own personal impressions or findings.

Office or workplace

Finding somewhere to do your meditation or Breath of Peace exercise during a break in the workplace might seem impossible at first, but be inventive. Where would you go for a break or rest or if you weren't feeling too well? Everyone's concentration levels drop after the first hour and a half of sitting, at a computer for example. After that, your body is seeking a space to regenerate some energy – hence the tea/coffee breaks. Lunch breaks are useful times and doing some meditation is more restful to your body than a catnap. (With your eyes closed, nobody can really tell the difference.)

I predict that in the not-too-distant future, meditation rooms will be the norm in most working places. By then you may be teaching others!

Group meditation guidelines

Rather than meditate by yourself, you may like to organise a weekly get-together with a friend or friends. Try it out for at least four sessions, using the guidelines in this book and then review your situation. Four sessions generally reveal whether participants form a compatable group for further work. Try to keep to the same venue, rather than having to get used to the atmosphere of a different place each time. Keep the group small: up to five people. Three people can form a very good working number. Form a circle or sit around a small table placed in the centre of the group upon which a lighted candle can burn. In this way the energies of each person are better focused.

One person needs to act as leader – you can take it in turns if you like – so that you actually *start* the activity instead of chatting and talking about it all evening. It's very easy to get into discussions as you gather and then the meditation can be sidetracked or even forgotten. It can easily become a total intellectual exercise rather than the aim of a well-balanced experience.

Make a rule that you exchange greetings, settle into your chairs and go straight into the Breath of Peace and/or the relaxation procedure. Save the chatter until afterwards – share your experiences and discuss them if you wish, but respect each other's privacy and refrain from discussing any other group member's findings outside the group. Build an integrity into the group idea from the start. In this way you will support each other with trust.

To help you focus, why not make your own tape of the Breath of Peace, the relaxation sequence and any of the other exercises in the following chapters, but remember to speak very slowly and allow good pauses. Setting a timer for the meditation might be helpful at first. Make sure it has a gentle sound rather than an alarm.

When you have 'come back' and grounded yourselves after the meditation (see Chapter 3), don't speak to one another before you have recorded your experiences in your notebooks. These may take the form of impressions, symbols, colours or anything else. Everything you feel and 'see' has some relevance to you, so record it – even if you think it may be bizarre – put it in your journal under the appropriate date. In time, you will be surprised how much of what you have experienced makes sense – sometimes weeks, months or even years later!

After the meditating session, it is important to have something to eat and drink. It helps to align all the body's energies and grounds you, preventing any feelings of spaciness.

Finally, try not to eat a heavy meal *before* meditation. If you have come home from work, school or have been away and return 'starving', have a little something to settle you, (sorry – *not* alcohol), then get the meal organised and go off and do your meditation. You'll digest your meal so much better.

Points of view

Your own understanding of the outer, physical world and your inner worlds is *coloured* by the sum total of your beliefs and concepts in each moment. You bring this unique package that has developed thus far to every situation or challenge in your life. Some people close their minds to investigation or further possibilities because they are comfortable with their truth and stick with it despite later evidence to the contrary. Keeping an open mind doesn't mean you enter into accepting and believing everything at face value.

It entails always being in a state for *observing* every moment and your place in that moment whether you are in the outer, physical world or exploring inner space.

In the following situation we see a group of individuals demonstrating their points of view.

The Art Class

Imagine you enter a room with eleven other people and all twelve of you take your seats which have been placed in a circle around the subject to be drawn. The subject is a young girl – a stranger to the class – and she is seated on a cushion which is set upon a raised platform so that you can all see her at a comfortable eye level. She is facing east.

The subject is wearing blue jeans and a colourful sweater with a pink front, blue back, green left sleeve and yellow right sleeve. Her brown hair is short at the sides with a ponytail at the back but her fringe is blonde. She has a dimple in her chin, she wears an earring in her right ear only and she is barefoot.

The teacher allots three minutes to observe her without allowing anyone to put pencil to paper and then suddenly he tells her to leave the room. He then gives the class another three minutes to write down a brief description of the girl as they saw her.

He then invites each person in the class to read out their descriptions one by one. This is what four of them say:

1   The person to the East is facing the girl and reports that she has short, blonde hair, is wearing a pink sweater with a green left sleeve and a yellow right sleeve. she has a dimple in her chin, wears one earring and is barefoot.

2   The person to the West is behind the girl and says she has long brown hair in a ponytail, is wearing a blue sweater with a green left sleeve and a yellow right one. She wears an earring.

3   The person to the South, on one side of her, reports that the subject has long, brown hair tied back in a ponytail with a blonde fringe, is wearing a pink and blue sweater with yellow sleeves, wears earrings and is barefoot.

4   The person to the North, on the other side of her, is colour blind. He reports that the girl has light hair tied back, she wore a grey-blue sweater, jeans and had bare feet. He thought she looked nice.

Have you noticed that in only four examples, each one of them has *assumed* certain things about the girl based on what they could see and that they also missed out some details. (For example, East assumed the girl was wearing a pink sweater because that's what he saw on his side.) You can check out more. At least each one of the four reported the girl was barefoot! (That may sound obvious, but it has been shown in tests of this kind that the observer can *invent* shoes and really believe they were worn!) You can see, however that by combining just these four descriptions out of the twelve in the class, we can get a reasonable picture of the subject, despite some lack of attention to detail from the four. Thus only one person (North) wrote down that she was wearing jeans, while South assumed she was wearing two earrings when only one could be seen.

Of course, we are merely demonstrating that each person in the room had a *different point of view* with differing abilities of observation. Each was coming from his or her space and observing from a different angle.

The art class turns out to be the art of observation, the art of non-assumption and the art of tolerance to your own and others' points of view.

We all have a valuable, individual viewpoint which improves with awareness, observation and practice wherever we are – physically active in the outer world, or journeying to our inner worlds. These two viewpoints of the outer and the inner self complement each other, grow together and develop together as you invest in regular meditation time, whether you are meditating in a group or alone.

Eventually, the mind expansion you develop through practising the creative meditations later on in this book will enable you to shift your focus on the inner plane to 'see' another's point of view and also experience how that feels. You can then bring this skill into the outer world. Everything begins and comes from within – from your inner nature. This is the gift of freedom of spirit awakening.

2
Who am I?

The art and practice of meditation provides a bridge between physical existence and the personal inner spaces

'*Know thyself*' – These words, inscribed on the Delphi temple in Greece long ago, give a clear directive to the seeker.

In order to further our investigation into what creative meditation offers you as a seeker, we need to outline the whole package of mind, body and spirit to get a clear and thorough idea of the tools with which we are working. Whether you just wish to use the guidelines for creating peaceful space and relaxation, or develop and explore extra-sensory and self-healing abilities, or understand your divinity and connect yourself to Universal Knowledge – whatever the motive – it is better to grasp the greater picture in the beginning so as to focus on your own particular area of interest or need later on.

If you watch a person meditating, all you see is someone seated with their eyes closed. Sometimes they may breathe deeply, make sounds of humming or chanting, but for the most part they sit peacefully. To the observer, this could appear quite boring. But wait – what are they doing exactly, what are they thinking or where is their consciousness or awareness?

If you were the meditator, only you would know the answers – except that we can generally describe the activity as *exploring inner space* or *inner landscapes*. The most natural shift in consciousness happens when we go to sleep and other shifts occur when we dream.

To become successful in tapping and understanding the wisdom and truths to be found on these inner levels *without going to sleep*, is accomplished simply by constant practice – in the same way as we learn to do anything in the physical world, like swimming, riding a bicycle or driving a car.

Of course, the vehicle for meditation is our own *body* – with *mind* and *spirit* operating too – all at the same time – although we perhaps may not fully realise this in hum-drum daily life. Yet, when under stress, we find ourselves saying words like 'I'm working hard just to keep body and soul together!' or 'I'm falling apart' or 'I'm going to pieces!' Somewhere in our consciousness and feelings, we are acknowledging the many intangible parts of ourselves.

To increase our knowledge or remind ourselves of the mind, body, spirit vehicle that we truly are, let's have a look at the body first. We already know that the *physical body* is an amazing and unique package of anatomy and physiology. This is but the first of a number of other bodies which complete our 3D spacesuit for experiencing life on planet Earth.

There are another eight bodies, called *subtle bodies*, so-called because they are composed of finer substance than physical matter; and since they resonate and vibrate at a finer frequency, they inter-penetrate the physical body and radiate around it. Because we look at everything from a physical, third-dimensional viewpoint, the subtle bodies are invisible to ordinary sight, except to those people who have extra-sensory abilities or who have developed them. They can 'see' or 'feel' these colourful emanations around the physical body which form an oval shape called the *aura* (see diagram).

The aura generally extends about a metre around the physical body. It is constantly moving, changing and expressing, with colours, the state of health and emotions of its owner, due to the actions and reactions of both the various bodies and the vortices of energy called *chakras*. (We will examine these later.)

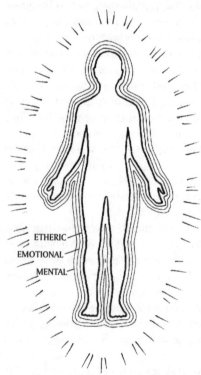

ETHERIC
EMOTIONAL
MENTAL

The aura, showing the radiation from three of the subtle bodies

Nowadays, more and more people are able to see this electromagnetic field by using technology such as Kirlian photography or on a video screen connected to an electrocrystal scanner used over the physical body.

The subtle bodies

With the wealth of information available today, we may find variations in the names that identify the many subtle bodies, largely because, after the first three or four, the remainder are operating as finer, spiritual vehicles whose names may vary because of different cultures and traditions. Different names can be initially confusing to the seeker so we will only identify the first few subtle bodies to keep our understanding simple and useful for our meditation purposes.

The *physical, etheric, emotional* and *mental* are known as the *lower bodies* of our third-dimensional spacesuit. The remainder are known as *higher bodies* since they vibrate at finer (higher) frequencies.

The first emanation from the physical body is called the etheric body. It radiates about an inch away from the skin as a bluish-white light. Most people can see this around others if they ask them to stand/sit against a plain wall – especially when daylight is poor or there is candlelight available. The following points highlight its role:

1 The etheric body holds the blueprint of your whole physical body.
2 Its vitality reflects that of the physical body.
3 Its condition, is directly related to the state of your physical, mental, emotional and spiritual health.
4 Illnesses collect here before manifesting in the physical. (Healing this body in time can usually save a great deal of suffering.)
5 Its normal strong lines of radiance are easily affected by magnets and crystals.
6 Radiation of any kind can de-vitalise it.
7 Accidents, surgery, drugs, emotional traumas or an abusive lifestyle bring damage, holes or tears which can affect its power.
8 'Hands-on' healing and massage feed it energy. Therapeutic touch balances it.
9 The etheric body is the physical body's energy (life-force) matrix and is particularly connected to the Astral/emotional body.
10 The *Soul* is connected to the etheric body.

The emotional body enables us to experience emotion, desire, joy and love as well as all the opposite – lower, depressing, negative emotions. There are seven levels to this body: the lower levels deal with personal fears and insecurities and the higher ones link to wisdom and truth. The following points highlight its role:

1   The emotional body is also able to sense vibrations that your other bodies can't.
2   The connecting point on the physical body is the solar plexus area.
3   This body is continually recording everything you experience from your point of view into what is called an Akashic record or a file: your beliefs, memories and karma (the summary of all your actions through the law of cause and effect). These records are actually impressed upon your DNA.
4   Hidden, repressed emotional energies are held in the muscles and may be felt as heaviness, heat, coldness or oppressive, dark sensations.

Ancestral and other memories are often inherited with the physical body, causing a lack of freedom in the expression of true power due to blockages of negative, judgmental energies.

This is an interesting point of view regarding our ancestors, where the saying, 'The sins of the fathers are visited on the children' can allude to genetic patterns being passed on as well as their emotional traumas. For example, anything traumatic that happened to your mother when you were in the womb was also experienced by you and could have been registered in your emotional field.

With the far wider healing knowledge and understanding available today, it is possible for people to discover, acknowledge and heal or have healed, any negative, judgmental or traumatic blockages or legacies left by their forefathers. By taking this action on the physical plane, a healing occurs on all levels of existence and the negative ancestor pattern is lifted. A very profound act. (More in Chapter 8 on self-healing.)

Meditating can provide an initial platform for gently uncovering and releasing any unwanted and unnecessary emotional baggage.

The emotional body displays the most colourful band of energies in the aura. Sometimes the emotional body is called the *astral body*. In a sense it is – because it has such a deep connection to the emotionly-sensitive area of the solar plexus and therefore our emotional field, but to save confusion we can describe it as a spiritual vehicle which holds the *total* physical pattern and memory of who you are. It is the 'twin' of your physical body and is positioned as part of the etheric body field. It operates quite naturally, only without the encumbrance and heaviness of the physical body.

On occasion, some people have seen an astral/etheric double when the right conditions have prevailed. It is often either a living or 'deceased' relative or someone close to them.

The astral body enables you to fly free from the physical body to the astral planes (described later in this chapter: see Spirit Section), which we often visit and experience through dreams. The consciousness is transferred from the physical to the astral body when the physical is at rest. Out-of-the-body experiences (OOBEs) are called astral projections and can happen involuntarily or naturally while you are awake.

(It is not wise to attempt this consciously without experienced advice, for it can lead to difficulties under certain circumstances where your body becomes, momentarily, open to undesirable, negative influences which can invade your space and seek to share your Life Force! This state of affairs of being 'bugged' is all too common when people experiment without preparation.)

The astral body is connected to the physical body by a silvery cord of infinite elasticity which breaks only when it is the right time to drop the physical body (die). When we awaken after a night's sleep, our astral body slips back into alignment in our physical body quite safely and naturally. Sometimes we may remember where we have been – usually we don't!

To be awakened suddenly, or to be subjected to sudden jolts or to leap out of bed in the morning is not good news for the astral body, since the alignments with your physical body could be affected, so that you are 'off centre' for the rest of the day, which manifests as 'shock', perhaps dizziness, grumpiness or a headache. A few minutes of meditational practice should put things right for this kind of situation.

Note that when we practise creative meditation, we are are using our mental, higher mental and other spiritual/Soul bodies in a protected, altered state of consciousness so that higher dimensions and higher wisdom can be accessed.

The art and practice of meditation provides a bridge between physical existence and the higher dimensions of the Universe.

The mental body tends to display a faint yellow hue. It is the vehicle for contacting thoughtwaves on multi-dimensional levels (Universal Mind).

It is the thinking body which relates to the bony structure of the physical body. It can hold on to judgments and have rigid attitudes of negative, unyielding thoughts which can eventually manifest in skeletal disorders. Emotional matters with connections to such feelings as anger, fear, guilt and grief, start as mental impulses which move into the emotional body. Since thought is instantly converted into feelings and vice-versa, so the two bodies, emotional and mental, are always interacting.

To recap: the physical, etheric/astral, emotional, mental bodies are called the lower bodies. the remaining spiritual bodies are called the higher bodies. All nine bodies are within the capsule of the aura which grows as you develop your spiritualty. The chakras are also included within the aura (see below). This capsule is your 3D space-suit. The grounding device is the physical body which is a person's own sacred laboratory space for conducting Life Force experiments!

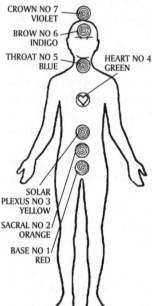

CROWN NO 7 VIOLET
BROW NO 6 INDIGO
THROAT NO 5 BLUE
HEART NO 4 GREEN
SOLAR PLEXUS NO 3 YELLOW
SACRAL NO 2 ORANGE
BASE NO 1 RED

The seven chakras

The chakras

As you may already know, the word 'chakra' is a Sanscrit word for a moving wheel or vortex. This describes what they look like as points of greater electromagnetic activity within the Aura. They don't operate as part of the physical body but are connected to it through the spinal system and the endocrine glands. There are a great many of these vortex points connected to the body, but for our meditation purposes we need first to observe the seven major chakras and the minor ones in the hands and feet (see diagram). Later on, we will incorporate five more chakras which exist above the body into our creative meditation system.

Chakras mediate all energy within the body, coming out of and going back into the body, and help to distribute energy for our physical and also our mental, emotional and spiritual functions, described previously as our subtle bodies.

In a way, they are rather like storage batteries. Each chakra works its purpose for a particular area of the body, front and back – all spinal problems are linked to an original block in the relevant chakra and presents a weakness through which the spinal or back problems surface. The frequencies that can be absorbed or projected through the chakras are transmitted into the vertebrae of the spine, transferred along nerve pathways to the organs or tissues etc. to which they are linked.

Each chakra has a number, name, colour, sound and position relating to the part of the body associated with it. The colours are the seven colours of the rainbow.

Each chakra works with the physical body and all of the subtle bodies all the time, whether we are aware of this or not.

Don't worry if you think that this background information is unnecessary for you, or that you might not be able to assimilate it at this stage. The information is here so that you can refer back to it if necessary, especially if you are interested in self-healing. Later on, the meditation practice exercises will show how it all falls into place very easily.

To help you identify yourself with the chakras, here is a description of them and some of their levels of function (see diagram):

1. **Base. Red. Pelvic area. Coccyx (at base of spine).** Concerned with circulatory, reproductive and elimination systems. Life force centre involved with basic survival which connects us to all different environments. Our quality of security relates to the success of mastering positive survival techniques. Negative blocks are: feeling separated, insecure, needing approval, acting without thinking, craving excitement/diversions, constant activity, physical and sexual, and being manipulative. Awareness of past life talents is rooted here. The last chakra to be healed before enlightenment.

2. **Sacral/spleen. Orange. Lower abdomen.** Concerned with muscular system, spleen, pancreas, bladder and kidneys. Deals with relating to others (relationships) and personality functions. Challenges: Inability to get along with others, worrying what others think of you, the

values of social status, power-seeking, overloading on pride and arrogance. Distorted programming re male/female images and their roles, perhaps as an inheritance from ancestors or from negative, childhood experiences.

3. **Solar plexus.** Yellow. Above and below waistline. Particular links to the astral, emotional and mental bodies. Concerned with digestion of food and assimilation of nutrients, the stomach, liver, gall bladder, intestines. Connects to left hemisphere of the brain.

Challenges: Denial of self-worth, denial of true nature by creating an artificial self to live by, denial of power by leaving things for other people to deal with. Eating indigestible foods including cravings to satisfy the palate not for energising the body. The state of health is enlightened when this chakra is balanced and charged.

4. **Heart.** Green (also linked to Pink). Heart area. Linked to the arms and lungs. The central chakra of the seven. Connected with all heart functions, body's circulatory system, thymus gland, immune system, tissue regeneration. Connects to right hemisphere of the brain. As the central, mediating chakra of the body, it receives Life Force and circulates it to every cell. The power here is love and compassion. Challenges: Learning to accept and integrate all parts of ourselves by finding the ability to love, understand and feel compassion for the self and others. Blocks or restrictions here affect the entire immune system and tissue regeneration processes.

5. **Throat.** Blue. Throat/mouth areas. Influences thyroid and parathyroid glands, mouth, teeth, throat: bronchial and vocal, respiratory system. Throat problems: soreness, tonsillitis, thyroid etc. indicate some blockages where a resistance to expressing one's own creativity is manifesting. The right-hand hemisphere of the brain and creative functions of the mind are tied to this chakra. The consciousness opens to telepathy and deep insight when stimulated.

6. **Brow.** Indigo (deep dark blue/hint of violet). Forehead (third eye), eyes, ears, face. Connects to the endocrine and immune systems, sinuses and ears. The qualities of the will and intellect, creative visualisation, imagination and higher vision are sited here and developed by meditational work. Unites the right eye (male aggressiveness) and left-hand brain function (analytical thought), with the left eye (female passivity) and right-hand brain function (art: patterns, colour, images, symbols, music). (See also 'Mind' section.) The brow is the centre for higher clairvoyance, opening to a higher spiritual vision.

7. **Crown.** Violet. Top of the head. Link with the physical self to the spiritual self. Connected to nervous system: all nerve pathways. Brain function, particularly the pineal and pituitary glands. The whole skeletal structure. When this chakra is poorly developed, there are limits to attaining true balance even though there may be many intellectual abilities and knowledge. This creates a restriction in connecting with the primary Soul Path (your true earthly mission). Its job is to create perfect synchronicity between all the chakras, but particularly between the heart, throat and head. When development takes place, this can be a doorway to investigating past lives and the subtle bodies can be balanced and purified.

Creative meditation work with the chakras enables mind control, through visualisation, to direct the thoughts and breath to align the chakras, which creates a safe, peaceful opening for divine illumination and healing to come through, into and down from the crown chakra. The top three chakras eventually synchronise, creating the 'halo' effect around the head, but it is equally important to work in bringing down healing illumination to all the chakras right down to the base – the last to heal – and thus to the whole self.

Meditating with this process brings peace, healing and enlightenment into your living, third-dimensional reality and the proof manifests in gradually feeling the effects as a lighter, healthier and more wise being. The following strengths occur when the full Creator Force is brought into the chakras of the third-dimensional body: To the first chakra: power in operating in your environment (security). To the second chakra: power in relating/relationships with others. To the third chakra: power in selfhood/Life Force (health). In the fourth chakra, we integrate this power of experience with love, to harmonise and balance it with compassion, resulting in acquiring wisdom. The fifth chakra – the communicating chakra – becomes a full creative expression by now having the ability to combine the power of the lower chakras with the love, compassion and acquired wisdom of the heart. In the sixth chakra, where vision develops, and in the seventh chakra of unification, all the strengths really come together: power, love/harmony, wisdom and creativity.

This maturing process unfolds naturally, through living and gaining the experiences which are outlined by each chakra, and occurs whether you are conscious of it developing in this way or not.

When a person decides to ask and investigate the question 'Who am I?' you can see the tools for investigation and enquiry are all in place, just waiting to be revealed. Working with the tools brings greater understanding and focus to the purposes behind the hardships and lessons of life. These experiences – all those difficult and joyous things we go through – are clarified from the inner level to the outer, physical level. It is then that your true path (Primary Soul Mission) and the meaning of your life can be accessed. The chakra system is a major key for this journey.

Mind

You are what you think you are.

Mind can tend to be an elusive subject when trying to bring it into a context for everyday living. It's not enough to say it just *is* – although that is the truth of the matter!

There are regular, intellectual and sometimes scientific discussions on radio and television which try to analyse what the mind is and does. Once you start to meditate on a regular basis, you will probably be able to recognise people who don't, for analysis is a function of the left-hand hemisphere of the brain. When you hear people analysing something intensely with only facts and figures, you know instantly that they haven't been where you have and explored a greater picture.

The brain is the physical, third-dimensional tool for the mind. Our mental and higher mental bodies are the subtle bodies which work with the mechanics of the physical brain and body. They can link us through their frequency and mental energy to the minds of other people on this our third-dimensional plane, and also to other dimensions through our extra-sensory, telepathic skills. We are therefore, all part of the Universal Mind or as some call it – *all that is* – whether we consciously use these frequencies or not, recognise them or not – or decide to clean up our circuits and get really plugged in through meditating!

The power of the brain

To try to understand the mechanics behind mind and meditation, let's briefly examine the hemispheres of the brain.

The left brain hemisphere deals with the physical world, logic, reasoning, linear thinking, mathematics and skills of speech (language) as well as scientific skills, organisational and analytical abilities, coding memory in verbal (linguistic) description. When working by itself, it can be over-analytical, judgmental and cannot remember what it learns, so repeated learning ensues.

The right brain hemisphere deals with the spiritual world, intuition, imagination, inspiration, insight, instinct, creativity, colour and language expressed in patterns and symbols – coding memory in images. When working by itself, information comes via the senses, but there is an inability to use or express this creatively.

When the two hemispheres work together spontaneously, the bridge between them is clear connecting neurological pathways, which enable left-hand brain learning to become internalised. We are then able to listen, remember and think, communicating information, thoughts and feelings in a creative way. The use of negative words – which is really negative programming – can switch off the right-hand hemisphere. Positive speech and affirmations will result in synchronicity, creativity and manifestation.

When we meditate, there is a measurable shift in the brainwave patterns and therefore it may be useful to know how to identify these. Brainwave rhythms are expressed in cycles per second (CPS):

Beta: The level of the conscious mind in the physical world operating with the physical senses of sight, sound, smell, taste and touch. Starts at 14 CPS, averaging usually around 21 CPS. Can rise to 25–30 CPS when a person is excited.

Alpha: The level of the inner conscious mind, the spiritual world connecting to the higher (or divine) mind and also intuition. During this creative, meditative, day-dreaming/thinking state there is cell energy renewal, some ESP (Extra Sensory Perception) and the beginning of suggestibility for the sub-conscious mind – no time or space. Ranges from 7–14 CPS.

Theta: The level of a deeper connection to inner consciousness where we tap into higher consciousness levels and states of peace and bliss. This level activates a deeper state of ESP. It initiates powerful levels of suggestibility which are used in various ways such as painless dentistry, surgery and childbirth. This is the beginning level of psychokinesis (PK), which means moving objects by 'will': mind over matter. A target level for practitioners of 'remote viewing'.

Delta: The level of deepest sleep/unconscious state, during which all ESP and PK talents are stimulated and where the qualities of total memory and total suggestibility are instilled, e.g. in the control of pain and bodily sensations for surgery, dentistry and childbirth.

The rhythms are *not* synchronised in the two hemispheres of the brain in ordinary people.

During the practice of meditation, however, the beta rhythms of ordinary daily existence drop to a slow alpha frequency and at the same time, the rhythms become synchronous in the two hemispheres. It has been found that when meditation has been practised regularly over a long period, the synchronicity persists even in the waking state. (Some years ago, tests done on psychics and healers revealed strong alpha and even theta rhythms during their waking states).

To summarise: observation of the workings of the two hemispheres of the brain and the brainwave rhythms shows very simply that if we gradually expand the mind through meditation, we can access many other dormant abilities. We can expand our point of view through the power of the mind.

There are four recognised levels to describe the function of the total mind: the *conscious*, the *subconscious*, the *unconscious* and the *superconscious*. We use the conscious mind for reasoning and for the interpretation of signals from the senses in order to make decisions in everyday life. It is the egotistical self – the we show to the world through speech and words. The subconscious mind has a memory bank of belief systems, habits, attitudes and fears, formed with childhood conditioning and environmental influences and it acts upon these and other instructions programmed into it by the conscious mind. The unconscious mind works all the time, non-stop on chemical and electrical impulses to build the physical body to maintain and repair it. The language it knows comes from genes and instructions handed on from the subconscious. The superconscious mind has superior mental powers, the highest aspect of the total mind which is called the Higher Self. This is the source of everything you need or may need to know. Telepathy is its vehicle of communication through inspiration, intuition and illumination.

The mind can bring anything creative into existence and it can also bring into existence many things that are not desired or desirable, simply through the ignorance of not being specific and positive.

The key is first to seek knowledge through the mind as to how to accomplish anything for the highest possible good, both for yourself and others. Don't buy into the fashionable notion that there is something outside yourself- out there – sometimes called fate, which operates as a random activity over which you have no control. *You are what you think you are*. What's it going to be then ?

Spirit

Spirit is the vehicle of the Soul. It can be basically understood as having many parts in the design of the 3D spacesuit: those invisible, subtle bodies we called the higher bodies are all of the higher spiritual nature. Spirit also resides in the lower bodies, particularly connected to the astral/emotional body.

We are therefore spiritual beings experiencing life in a temporary, physical body. Soul is the life expression system, enabling the spirit – the individual essence and identity within – to express itself on conscious, subconscious, unconscious and superconscious levels.

The Soul stores the experience of your present life while the memories of 'past' or other lives are withheld at birth into a new body. It also contains the Higher Self (one of your higher, spiritual bodies) which survives after death when all the other lower vehicles are jettisoned. Someone called it the Permanent Self because it really is permanent being contained within the Soul body which can move in space, move from one dimension to another and reside in a physical body from time to time to experience the world of matter. It uses the mask of a human body personality, which you are now, for that life's mission which we can call the Temporary Self, for it only exists for a single lifetime and is the lower ego. The most important first connection to make is with the Higher Self/Permanent Self – your guardian – through creative meditation. Eventually, when mind, Soul and spirit are blending together, the result is pure Soul energy.

More about the astral/etheric planes

For most people, when they die/drop the body, spirit carries the Soul in its astral/etheric body (which is a replica of how you look right now) to the next level of existence – the astral plane – which has seven levels divided into lower, middle and higher. The astral plane is similar to the physical plane except what we see is less stable, more fluid and can change shape. This is because astral and all higher dimensional 'substance' is capable of *taking any form that is impressed upon it*.

Here is another concept of mind power, where from the lower astral levels, distortions of truth, illusions and power games in the name of spirituality can be attracted by the unwary who dabble in curiosity. Conversely, with right intent and right preparation, higher frequencies of experience will be forthcoming. (The true seeker does not proceed solely out of idle curiosity – the sensation seeker does.)

Another difference operating on other dimensions is that time and space are not factors of limitation as they are in physicality in the third dimension, for time can be lengthened, stretched or condensed into moments. On Earth, there is a delay mechanism between thinking the thought and having it manifest because of the density of matter here.

Think beautiful thoughts
This is the way to blend body, mind and spirit. When you act (body), think (mind) and meditate for your highest possible good (spirit), your personal vibration changes and your thoughts travel faster on finer frequencies. Of course, this means you have a greater response-ability (ability to respond) in transmitting only the right thoughts. A bad thought transmitted is a bundle of low frequency energy – and as energy is always circular in motion, it eventually comes back to its source! Hence the saying 'What goes around, comes around'.

A good way to deal with this is to say 'I cancel that!' when you realise you are saying or thinking naughty things (these may be judgmental, critical, spiteful or wishful). Gradually, you will programme yourself into gracious silence and positive thinking.

If a person has behaved in what you consider to be an unforgivable way, then just realise that universal laws (see below) apply to everyone and that you can walk away, confident in the knowledge that the energy they projected to you will automatically and eventually return to them. Vindictiveness must be avoided even in the knowing. 'Getting your own back' really means that! It will return clothed in a slightly different way, involving you in more of the same – it pulls you back. Get wise – don't waste your valuable resources by getting hooked into this 'stuff'. Here is an indication of how the Power of Peace enters into the daily moment where we all have the response-ability, in order to help clean up our human dramas.

Once you move from the lower, emotional responses, you won't be bothered by them from others, for you will have moved on to better things.

You can understand how this works by noting some of the universal laws which are extensions of physical laws as they apply to the spiritual world. These laws are interconnected, so the totality of our body, mind, spirit capsule is served by them.

* Law of attraction: thoughts, words, deeds and feelings, produce like energies.
* Law of cause and effect: every action has a reaction. Negative attracts negative.
* Law of compensation: blessings and abundance come as a visible effect of our deeds through cause and effect.
* Law of correspondence: as above, so below. Principles of physics have correspondence in the Universe (etheric).
* Law of gender : balance of masculine/feminine polarities: basis for all creation.
* Law of perpetual transmutation: all people have within them the power to change conditions in life. Higher vibrations consume and transform lower ones.
* Law of polarity: law of mental vibration: change undesirable thoughts by concentrating on the opposite (balancing).
* Law of relativity: tests of initiation: the challenges in life are relative to the need to master them.
* Law of rhythm: seasons, cycles, patterns of development: mastering the flow through positivity.
* Law of vibration: everything vibrates, moving in circular fashion: thought, word and deed etc.

Everything in the Universe is energy which can be measured and reduced to vibrational frequency. *This includes every thought, word, emotion, experience, object and particle.*

I understand there to be twelve dimensions in this Universe. All have seven levels which hold their own frequency. It sounds complicated, but it does put third- dimensional thinking into perspective. You cannot 'see' the other dimensions because their energy is 'stepped up'. Looking through a telescope will not reveal to the viewer anything more than a development of third-dimensional understanding. With skill and practice, there are people who can journey in the mind to other dimensions and return with information, or through the Power of Peace in mind, body and spirit receive (channel) higher information or higher knowledge to help themselves and mankind.

Summary

The aura capsule encompasses our mind, body, spirit construct as a spacesuit for physical existence on a third-dimensional planet. In each section, large proportions are dysfunctional because they haven't been used and have gone to sleep! Once we start to wake up and look at the greater picture with as much balance as possible in choosing what is right for us at this time, we can begin to make connections of importance to ourselves. One of the first challenges is to (re)discover our Higher Self so that our primary path in life can unfold, no matter what our age. As we simply let the Power of Peace into every cell of our bodies we will then gradually begin to move into a position of attracting the right things and the right people into our lives at the right time.

3

Relax into meditation

The key to achieving personal harmony in meditation is through simple relaxation.

Now that we are more familiar with our 3D spacesuit and can put into place all the practical requirements of 'where' and 'when' for our meditations, we are finally ready to limber up with 'how'. Short, but deliberate relaxation exercises are essential at the start of meditation, especially for the beginner. We have to move from a state of perhaps tense, physical, mental or emotional activity in the outside world to a state of serenity which provides the required relaxed effect in our whole being in order to focus. This is often called being in a *state of relaxed concentration*. The objective is to quieten the body on all levels in order to accomplish the shift in consciousness to an alpha state or peaceful mode. Our concentration is then lifted above the happenings, irritations or worries of the day.

Tension is energy which is blocked instead of being released properly.

One of the most useless pieces of advice from well-meaning friends or loved ones is: 'Don't worry – relax!' This is guaranteed to increase your tension. Tension has many sources – mental, emotional and physical, and all three usually work as a total package.

Think of a runner at the starting block and the build-up prior to the awaited commands and the firing of the starting pistol. Mind, body and emotions are all geared to peak at the moment the runner springs forward. The ready, steady … go! Now think of the same runner, all energies focused at the starting block – the commands come, the gun fires and it fires again … false start! Oh, no! The build-up of tension falls away, the concentration wavers … and much of that energy implodes, for it has been ready for instant release and action.

You are running late for an important appointment and the traffic lights ahead are only allowing two or three cars at a time – waves of tension start to build within you … Scenarios similar to these occur all the time where a constant build-up of tension has to surface. It results in a range of reactions such as rage, anger, irritation, muscle cramp, stomach pain, frustration or tightness around the chest area.

Sometimes, grief is held within a person for years, stowed away and hidden deeply from the conscious mind. A reaction can be eventually triggered off by a local, national or international event which touches the masses. Everyone identifies in some way with the sadness. Perhaps personal memories are triggered, but often, the emotional atmosphere is enough to bring tears which flow naturally and the grief is released. Sometimes the effect can take people by surprise with no understanding from where it has really surfaced, its origins rooted long ago in the past.

Emotional/mental release is very health-giving, but there are times when it is expressed in totally outrageous and imbalanced ways. This is because there has been a build-up of tension over a long period and the event occurs which has the right ingredients to act as a trigger for the release.

All events happening 'outside', which we observe as coming 'at us', in which we are involved or become involved by reaction, are mirrors of something we need to observe, experience and try to understand. We have actually attracted them for this purpose.

Once you can truly understand the role of your response-ability despite the prevailing difficulties, you are proving your self-worth and integrity.

When a state of serenity is achieved in meditation, if only for short periods at first, there is a developing ability to respond in the outside world with wisdom. If you have been undergoing immense mental or emotional stress in your life or you are following a strong medication programme for health reasons, the Breath of Peace and the following suggestions for relaxing prior to meditation, could help in de-stressing your body; but don't continue into any of the other options of the full meditation programme at this time on your own. (If you can, have a therapeutic massage from a qualified person so the stress can be released from the muscles of the physical body to start getting you into recovery.)

Relaxing before meditation

Try yawning three or four times for tiredness and tension but try to breathe mostly through the nose, not the mouth. This is also a good tip for the voice since it will prevent overstraining the larynx.

Dropping the lower jaw and placing the tip of the tongue behind the lower teeth relaxes the face muscles. Taking a deep breath in and letting the breath out from the mouth, making the sound 'pow, pow, pow ...', also achieves a quick release of tension. (A good idea in stressful traffic conditions!)

Blinking the eyes several times cleanses and rests them, as does looking from near to far, say from a computer screen to the clouds in the sky or from a reading a book to looking into the distance.

If you suffer any illness temporarily, such as a cold, cough or influenza, try only the preparation and breathing exercises. A few minutes of peaceful, breathing meditation is very healing to your whole system and your rate of concentration isn't likely to fund a longer session into creative meditation anyway. Here are three ways to relax before meditation:

a   By breathing: *Power of the Breath*.
b   Listening to peaceful sounds of nature or delicate music which act upon the mental and emotional levels: *Power of Peaceful Sounds*.
c   Receiving directions from someone or giving ourselves directions to relax each part of the body: *Power of Command*.

All three can be either done separately or combined.

a) Power of the Breath

As stated in Chapter 1, the breath is the most important of tools for meditating and is the creative link which generates everything you do in the meditative state.

There are very few people who physically breathe properly; consequently, respiratory diseases are very common. (Perhaps our bodies are trying to close down from the various pollutants found in our atmosphere.) If you take up physical exercise of any kind, including walking, you know how much better your body feels after some fresh air. At least it's the one vital commodity which is free to everyone – at the moment!

Apart from air keeping us alive and oxygenating the blood – properly air-conditioned blood is happy blood – there is another unseen factor that we in the western world have begun to realise more and more. Through the breath we connect to *prana* or the Life Force energy that feeds the Soul. This is an ancient Sanskrit word describing this energy that is breathed in – something that has been known for centuries by many races, particularly those in the Far East.

Prana can be stored in the body. It creates a forcefield of vitality for all the nine bodies of our 3D spacesuit. If you ask scientists what is in the element air that you can label 'prana', you may not receive an agreeable answer, unless of course, they are familiar with ancient knowledge.

Breathing for health

Wherever you are at this moment, try to focus on your breath – listen to yourself breathing. Don't force your breathing – just breathe normally and rhythmically. In fact, imagine you are doing this in *slow motion* to get the idea of a relaxed approach. Close your eyes to help concentration.

Exercise 2: Power Breathing

Feel the breath coming through your nostrils as cool ... and the breath out as warm ... and again ... and again ... 3 times. Now breathe in ... to the count of 3 and stop. Hold the breath for 1 ... 2 ... 3 counts and now breathe out through the mouth ... to the count of 4. Stop ... hold the breath in ... pause to the count of 4. The pattern is 3–3–4–4: breathing in to 3, holding for 3, breathing out for 4, and pausing for 4 counts. Repeat this sequence initially at least 6 times. On following days, extend to 9 times, then 12 times as you feel comfortable. The idea is to gradually build towards a 3-minutes session for this exercise. For just those few moments you have been concentrating on your breath quite easily and thus controlling other thoughts from entering your mind, as you did when breathing the Breath of Peace. By holding the breath in a voluntary way just for a few seconds, you begin to take more control over your physical vehicle. At this point, don't hold the breath any longer than suggested. Be comfortable and maintain focus.

Now close your eyes again and repeat the above sequence noticing where your breath reaches as it comes through your nostrils. Pull it in a bit further *very gently*, as if it reaches another doorway, the first being at the back of the nostrils, the second and third deeper in. (By the way, avoid breathing *in* through the mouth at all times.) You'll notice *where* you are breathing most of the time – what your breathing habit pattern is, and you'll be able to feel where slow, deeper breathing reaches, if and when your ribs (lungs) expand.

Experiment with this and get to know the power you are controlling and directing. (So many of us have been shallow breathers for most of our lives, not realising we have deprived our bodies of a natural intake of vitality.) Shallow breathing also occurs because of tense nostrils which can be rectified by dilating them on the inward breath. Combine this wide nostril in-breathing with out-breathing through the mouth, because, since we breathe out toxins from the body all the time and we also breathe out tension, it will achieve more than one benefit.

Use the following exercise as part of your limbering up to relax *before* meditation, or as a breathing meditation in itself.

Exercise 3: Relax and Detox (Campfire) Breathing

Light the candle in front of you. Mentally ask that this light surrounds your aura, your whole being and your sacred space. Sit comfortably on your chair, hands lightly resting on the thighs. Close your eyes. Imagine you are sitting on your chair in the open air in a peaceful, walled garden, quite secure and relaxed. It is a still, warm evening. On the ground in front of you, about 1–2 metres away is a small campfire. This is your own personal campfire – it is burning clearly with no smoke and with red, blue and violet flames. The candle that you lit earlier is a symbol which represents the campfire. As you breathe in, open the nostrils. Open the mouth to breathe out. As you breathe in you know you are breathing vibrant, clear air which is sustaining your body – you are 'drinking in' a special air elixir through your nostrils which feeds you positive energy. As you breathe out through your mouth, you are breathing out all the toxic, negative energy from your body, aiming directly towards your campfire. The fire with its colours of red, blue and violet will absorb all the toxic waste you breathe out and transmute it and purify it. Breathe slowly and rhythmically. As the out-breath comes out, don't blow it – just let the air leave you as if you are letting go or sighing. You can make this sound of sighing with every out-breath. Begin to see, in your mind's eye, the fire collecting, consuming and transmuting each of your out-breaths encompassed with your sigh. Don't forget, you are widening the nostrils for each in-breath in order to take in the full quality of air elixir.

Continue for several minutes or as long as you feel is right for you. You can either sit quietly observing your campfire for a period of peaceful contemplation or close down now. When you are ready to return, please observe this simple closing down procedure: Say to yourself 'I am now closing down'. Count down from 7 to 1. These numbers represent your seven chakras system from the crown (head) to the base (seat). As you say the numbers, be aware that each chakra is then closed. Then feel your feet on the ground and direct a deep breath into your feet and into the ground itself. Open your eyes and stretch. Take some deep breaths and without talking (to group members if present), write down any impressions. (The full closing down procedure is given in Chapter 4. Since you have the option to do this exercise as a breath detox or continue on into a peaceful contemplation, I have recommended this simple close down here, as a natural precaution so that you can come back to full consciousness slowly, remain centred and protected.)

During meditation our breathing does change automatically into a quieter, slower rhythm, so we don't really notice it unless we are directing it somewhere. It is *where* we focus our attention for the breath coupled with imagination or visualisation that brings you more power to accomplish your intent.

b) Power of Peaceful Sound

The right choice of a tape for background music is important. Be very discerning. As stated earlier, the sounds of nature – birds singing, water falling over stones or sounds of the seashore – are those to employ. On the whole, these sounds won't encroach on your concentration but will bring a sense of relaxation. There is a small problem in that one can become too reliant on sound to divert the attention and that later on it can interfere with some inner observations; this is why natural sounds are best. Nevertheless, it is a helpful 'prop' and can set the scene for peaceful relaxation.

When making your own tapes from the exercises in this book as instruction for yourself or your group, you can also speak the words into your tape while another tape plays appropriate sounds/music in the background. In this way, a useful sound tool is created. Needless to say, it should be playing very softly behind your voice. (An in-depth look at the subject of sound in all its forms will be found in Chapter 9).

c) Power of Command

This is a well-known exercise for relaxing the body but very effective when extended as a way into mind power. It is easily done by yourself – even easier to listen to a tape, especially if you're a beginner.

The simplicity of telling each part of the body to relax can sound ridiculous at first, but it is these messages which are received by the subconscious which are at the root of the effectiveness of the exercise.

The subconscious mind is a databank of all you have experienced and learned. It controls every particle of your physical body, reacting on your conscious, everyday, thinking, reasoning mind. This control *only* operates through the instructions it receives from the conscious mind. The stronger the thought and the identification with an image suggested, the quicker the subconscious will react and comply with your instructions. This is a simple explanantion of mind-training – that is, training the sub-conscious with your thoughts.

Do you remember when we looked at brainpower in Chapter 2? It explained that the use of negative words can switch off the right-hand hemisphere. Self-programming like this occurs with utterances or thoughts such as: 'I'll never be able to do that! ... I'm not good enough ... I can't do ... I'm unlucky ... I always fail at ...' etc. Of course, *positive* self-programming instructs the subconscious mind as well – you send your command down-line and the subconscious responds. The greater the emphasis given and with the repetition of the commands, the greater the effect is logged into your system and action follows. (Later on, you will see the value of affirmations.)

It is the conscious, thinking mind which sifts what it will and will not take on board, so if there is a negative mode with attitude, then that message is replayed throughout your system. It is the *belief* that you have confidence in your intent that ensures success.

An open mind is one that allows all possibilities to be considered. Therefore, *you are what you think you are.*

When we apply this to commanding the body to relax, there is a distinct physical reaction in all of your systems, to bring about an effect. There is a build-up of effectiveness as you do the following exercise more and more. When the subconscious receives new data input, sometimes there is a reaction if a person holds a lot of negative programming, particularly if there are previously held ideas about meditation, relaxation or allied subjects. Remember, you are still in control when relaxed because you are instructing yourself so to be. That gives you freedom to explore further.

Exercise 4: Power of Command Relaxation

Make sure you will not be interrupted. Prepare your sacred space by lighting your candle with the instruction that it is a symbol of peace and protection to you and the space all around you.

Sit comfortably in your chair with the hands resting lightly on your thighs, feet flat on the ground. Close your eyes and let your body settle down. Breathe peacefully ...

(Don't forget to speak slowly and clearly into the tape recorder, taking suitable pauses if you are taping this for your own use.) Become more and more relaxed into your chair, letting the chair support all of your weight. Feel your back, seat and thighs being supported by the chair ... feel your feet supported by the ground and grow long, golden roots from the soles of your feet into the ground ... deeper and deeper ... you are not going to sleep but relaxing the body, with the mind alert. Starting at the feet and going up the body: relax the feet – every bone and muscle in the feet is more and more relaxed ... relax the ankles ... all around the ankles. Relax the lower legs, relax the calf muscles ... relax the knees, and now relax the thighs ... every bone and muscle in the thighs ... more and more relaxed... sink deeper and deeper into your chair ... more and more relaxed in the body but staying alert in the mind. Let your tummy muscles relax ... relax the trunk of your body ... relax the chest ... relax the shoulders ... let all the stress and tension of the day flow down your body and into the ground ... more and more relaxed ... relax your arms down to the elbows ... now relax the arms from the elbows down to the wrists ... relax the hands ... relax your fingers and thumbs, right down to the tips ...

Bring your focus up to the nape of the neck ... relax the neck area ... and now the spine ... relaxing all the bones and muscles in the spine ... slowly relax down to the waist ... relaxing the spine from the waist down to your seat ... sinking into the chair... more and more relaxed ... relaxing the body but staying alert in the mind ... not going to sleep. Let the peace flow down your spine ... into your legs and down into the ground ... bring your focus up to your face ... relaxing the jawline ... the mouth and the cheeks ... relax the eyes and the forehead, letting all tension go Now relax the top of the head ... remaining mentally alert but all the body relaxed ... all the body relaxed from the top of the head all the way down to the tips of the toes ... *go now to* ... At this point you are ready to direct yourself into your chosen subject for meditation or contemplation so there is a need to be clear about this aim *before you start*. Guidelines for a variety of explorations are set out in Part 2, 'Getting Started'.

You can also just sit quietly for a few minutes, listening to your breath and allowing your body to become accustomed to the whole idea of the approach to a peaceful state. Eventually, you will be able to command the body into relaxation and enter a place of stillness in seconds. Your programming to the subconscious being in place, together with your breathing knowledge, will ensure you are in command.

When you are ready to return it is very important to go through the full closing down procedure given in Chapter 4, as this is an exercise which can take you well into the alpha state. If you find yourself going to sleep when you try this, then you are either too tired at the start and need to do more of the breathing exercises, or the induction is a bit slow or too long for you. (Of course, this is a good exercise for insomniacs if you leave out the 'don't go to sleep' command!)

Posture

One of the reasons that we sit with the spine upright for meditation (see diagram) is that breathing is easier. Another reason is that a most important flow of energy in the physical body is from the head and flows down the spine to its base (animals like being stroked downwards). You are then always in line with the Cosmos (spiritual) and the Earth (physical) and receptive to both.

When we lie down it is a signal to our bodies that we are ready for rest and sleep, and we are then parallel with the earth's surface. We have grounded our activities. This is *not* the right mode for meditating which, as we have already noted, is a state of relaxed body but focused mind.

I have emphasised the use of a chair with the feet on the ground because creative meditation uses the feet to ground the energies which can awaken in all the lower bodies during the various processes.

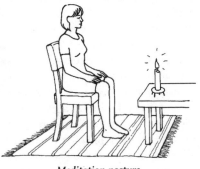

Meditation posture

(Incidentally, headache/tension in the head never escapes through the head. It needs to be breathed down the body to the feet and into the ground – see Chapter 8.) If you *have* to sit on the ground, make sure you are cross-legged and have a thick rug or cushion beneath you to prevent too much draining of your vital force into the Earth.

When sitting on the meditation chair, we place the hands with palms down on the thighs so that the physical body is well-aligned. (The right side of the body is the positive and the left side is the negative.) *Never* cross the feet or legs while relaxing/meditating, as this scrambles your body's energy flow. The head needs to be well-balanced with the eyes looking straight ahead as if looking into the distance. Aim to sit as comfortably as possible with your spine supported by the back of the chair and a cushion there if necessary.

Meditating is *not* about sitting stiffly upright and keeping still at all costs! (In the beginning, as you start, you may get an itch somewhere. If you do, scratch it, but do tell your body that you are in control and that it needn't agitate.) If you are disabled or in a wheelchair, try to do the best you can for your spine in keeping the upright position. Try not to fold your hands in your lap or over your stomach as this action inhibits or blocks that particular chakra. Before closing the eyes, spectacles, if worn, should be removed. It is also a good idea to take off any jewellery, watch, rings etc. Everything holds a frequency which could act as an inhibitor to your forcefield. Get rid of the trappings for a better tuning in. Lastly, always try to take off your shoes before meditation and wear extra socks for warmth if necessary.

The use of imagination promotes intuition and together they bring about inspiration.
Using visualisation (the imagination), we can consciously create many beneficial systems and scenarios to support ourselves in meditation, as we did with the breathing detox meditation and the campfire and then in a different way with the power of command sequence to relax the body. In this chapter, we have used this process in simple ways to bring about self-instruction, self-healing and body alignment (harmony) and for introducing the power of protection. This is explained fully in Chapter 4.

It is very easy to pre-judge and dismiss this power of creativity through the imagination, until you motivate yourself and experience these possibilities, many of which are designed ultimately to filter out into physical manifestation, depending on the intent and effect required (as in self-healing).

Some people have difficulties with visualising or creating a picture in their 'mind's eye'. This is perfectly natural so don't let it form a barrier to any of the exercises. Do them as written and know that the instruction acts on your inner levels bringing about the desired intent anyway.

Non-visual people are likely to be more enhanced in the 'feeling', 'sensing' or 'hearing' centres of the body, so this will be from where the major 'point of view' comes and through which intuition will develop. Most often, continued relaxation practice, in which the senses of touch, taste, smell and hearing are employed in the exercise, can bring about more development in the visual area, while at the same time the other senses develop more extra-sensory perception (ESP).

4
The power of protection

Switching on your power grid is illuminating.

This chapter is devoted to suggestions for general welfare when opening up to different ranges of frequency as can occur with meditation, any other research or, for that matter, enquiry employing the 'extra-senses'. Just as we wear protective clothing for difficult weather conditions or for certain jobs, so we need to know all about the possible conditions which prevail on other levels of existence (other dimensions) which can affect us, in order to prepare ourselves, or clothe ourselves, in the appropriate manner.

The simple fact to remember is that we need to maintain a good frequency – a good Life Force – which clothes the physical body inside and outside. On a purely physical level it means maintaining the immune system and only eating foods which have quality energy. On the subtle body and chakra levels, the maintenance can be assisted in many different ways through therapies which can help to release deep, negative blocks within; but currently, overwhelming evidence supports that it is through our meditational practices that a primary balance can be achieved. Here is an indication regarding the question of when and how many times a week we should do meditation. It is so good for you to get into the habit of regular meditation because it is nourishment for the system which builds up strength in the 3D spacesuit. We have looked at the entire spacesuit encapsulated in the aura, and within that, a simple version of how our brainpower works, outlining the power of the mind.

These areas describe the physical and non-physical parts of our being and are all covered by the use of mind (thought), which is employed to build the power of protection.

Of course, there are other tools that can enhance the environment in which we live or work and which can also help to uphold our bodies in harmony, such as the use of Feng Shui and the strategic placement of crystals, to name but two. Choose and create your own order and harmony around you in the ways that feel right for you; these will help to maintain your personal protection during meditations.

Everything has its place in the scheme of protection and enhancement in our environment. Some people have made the connection to the importance of harmony and others haven't.

It is a mistake to assume that it's all a bit 'unnecessary' if you haven't investigated and observed what is really going on. For example, the promotion of fear is one way of lowering the human energy field immediately. One way it is done on a mass scale is through horror movies, emotional and violent films and the peddling of negative news. As these thought-forms/ideas are registered on conscious and subconscious levels it can result in a programming of more fear in the human mind. Inevitably, these 'games' replay themselves through people and events in the outer, physical world over and over again as the same 'stress button' is pressed. Low-level astral energies feed off low-level physical energies such as radiation and emotional, fear-based thought-forms, thus creating an ever descending spiral. The level upon which your personal energy field is operating at any time (even by being simply overtired), can be open to attract the same. Like attracts like. When any manifestations occur which you observe or experience yourself, always ask, where and when did the original thought or idea come from? The event may have its roots that come from long ago in the past, which is set to replay throughout time unless the pattern is broken and cleaned up with the polarity energy required. Recurring wars are an example, where the polarity of peace is required.

In meditation or contemplation, you can promote the Power of Peace silently within yourself and gradually experience what that really means to every cell of your body. As you do this just for yourself, it radiates through your aura, affecting everything and everyone around you. It cannot fail if your intent is focused with no hidden agendas and no conditions. Like attracts like and gradually builds a protection and balances out any overload of negativity. It is so simple and a protection in itself. You may never know that your simple effort also had a profound effect somewhere else in the world.

It is worth noting here that the use of the word *occult*, merely meaning 'that which is hidden', is now used by some as a sinister term to denigrate or describe certain ideas as dubious practices in order to promote the growth of more fear. It was once a highly respected word denoting sacred knowledge, or hidden knowledge sometimes thousands of years old – quite different from the hocus-pocus now implied. Such is the fluidity of language in changing times. When the meaning of a word is changed, be alert. Ask yourself why and how this came about. Who promoted it? A changed word naturally changes the message and thus the attitude. In some cases, a sale of fear has been effected in a subliminal way.

Let us remain focused, however, on the development of our own inherent powers of protection and how to motivate and utilise them in a fear-based society by observing the following points:

1   Prior to meditation, it is very important to place a seal around and through your aura to protect your 3D spacesuit.
2   Every morning (perhaps as you clean your teeth so that you add this little ritual habitually), place the same protection around your aura and mentally around your children or family, if you have any. It needs a minimum of once daily. More is good.
3   The more you apply this rule, the stronger the protection – it builds up.
4   Whenever you are taking your body into challenging, crowded or unknown territory, the same thing applies – never mind whether you think it a suitable place or situation – still do it!
5   If you attend spiritual-type workshops, classes or meetings of any kind, there is no guarantee that your aura cannot be infiltrated by something – perhaps a dubious thought-form which can bring a sudden onset of weariness as it sticks to your aura. There are many jokers on the lower astral level who are attracted by the energy being emitted in such circumstances and events.
6   Make sure you don't exhaust yourself mentally, emotionally and physically. (Stress means you're giving away your power!)

By increasing the light and colour frequencies in and around your aura, lower frequencies cannot easily penetrate the shield of higher frequencies. As long as you maintain this and it becomes a natural habit, lower frequencies of all kinds of negative rubbish such as thought-forms, and lower astral entities, cannot attach easily to your life-support system. Like attracts like – simple fact, not fear.

As already mentioned, the human race is constantly putting out negative radiations through thoughts and all forms of communication, which, coupled with other radiations, e.g. from all electronic and technological equipment in our homes and our environment, combine to zap our energy big time. It is up to us, individually, to think carefully in a non-pollutant way and dedicate ourselves to the joy of living. Stop thinking what the other guys are doing and become creatively adaptable and more objective from within. Nurture yourselves first and teach your family.

Self-protection keeps up your energy field. Using your mind and breath, you are employing reason and logic (left-hand brain) with imagination and intuition(right-hand brain).

Rule 1: Protection Procedure

For the best effect and general use, the colours to imagine and use by way of the breath are scintillating white, with violet shades down to lilac and gold which can be used as a sealing device rather like the eggshell around the egg. Imagine and breathe what is called the *light* into the aura from above the head, around and through the body. You can do this anywhere – standing, sitting, under the shower, in the supermarket queue, in the train or in the car, but most of all just prior to meditation.

Focus on your position from within the centre of your aura capsule and say to yourself: *I place the light above me, below me, in front of me, behind me, to the left of me and to the right of me and all around me. I seal my aura with violet light and gold.* The term light, or white light, refers here to the colour spectrum perceived in its merged totality.

The seal of violet light is a powerful, protective device and is connected to these present times of the Age of Aquarius. As a new age filters through, it holds a particular colour ray to assist all life during and after the transition. The term violet light describes a merging of light with the colour violet which results in a shining lilac shade. It is very powerful and we find shades of it appearing every-where as a fashionable item. The combination of blue and red produces the purple, violet colour which, together with white light, creates a powerful transmuting, healing and protective ray.

Blue produces a calming, healing, cool effect, while red is stimu-lating and warm. When combined as violet, the effect on the human psyche is to enhance the ability towards meditation, contemplation or prayer with a specific purpose. It protects at the same time as it brings spiritual attunement by admitting outside impressions that you need or want to come to you, while shutting out the undesirable emanations. Violet-white light is the radiation of spirit tuned to *now*.

It is also interesting to note that reds give physical protection against disease. Yellow/orange, being colours of the intellect, protect you against another's argument or will, by enhancing your perceptiveness – your mind sharpens so that others' mental efforts will rebound from your aura. Blue protects your emotional nature, guarding you against others' emotions. It gives you immunity against lower, emotional desires directed at you by acting like an armour or shield. As you can see, the use of colour, by visualising or wearing it, can be so useful for different types of energy boosting and protection. We explore this in more detail in Chapter 9.

The Inner Column of Light

Have a look at the 3D spacesuit (aura) diagram showing the chakras 1–7 on the body and also showing the Soul Star about six inches above the head and the Earth Star six inches below the feet. The Soul Star and Earth Star are complimentary chakras – halves of the same whole, located as we see – outside the body, but within our 3D spacesuit.

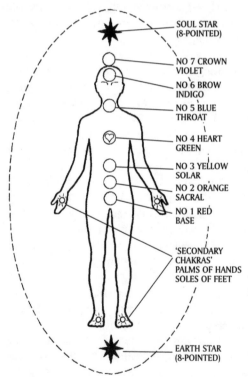

For meditation, they need to be connected to become fully operational, since the Soul Star is the place of your Higher Self/guardian which, long, long ago, resided within the physical body.

As man entered more and more into the experience of the density of the third

The 3D ('Third Dimensional') Space Suit

dimension, the Soul Star was separated to its present location above the body. This had the effect of almost completely closing down the physical body to its spiritual connections. Nearly everyone went to sleep concerning life beyond the third dimension.

Now everyone is waking up and feels change stirring. The turn of the millennium plays a part in finding humanity at the right time for new patterns to appear from the greater picture.

Now is the time when the Soul Star can be re-connected in a conscious way so that the primary Soul Path is gradually revealed through the presence of the Higher Self who is the guardian or gate-keeper of the 3D spacesuit. This is *the most important* connection to make, for it is your divine spark, your connection to the Cosmos and to the Source of All – the *direct* and *safe* route, to which you apply when requiring higher wisdom, clarity of purpose and guidance. (For some people, praying to God is how this might be interpreted. All explanations of this connection come in many forms according to beliefs and cultural traditions.)

Higher knowledge has always been available but is now pouring onto the planet through people making their connections. Your own understanding and pathway is unique to you and the wisdom of your Higher Self filters through what is right for you at the right time, depending on the intent and response-ability of the physical body. Remember, the physical body has the job of learning how to manage, survive and relate to the 3D environment while being cut off from source.

Once there is an awakening and the questions are asked, 'Who am I?', 'Where am I going?', 'What is going on?', the Soul Star light flashes and a response will be downloaded into the physical existence. It may be a book which falls off the library shelf in front of you. You meet someone who gives you a simple message. You tune in to a radio or television discussion programme. An evening class attracts you. Whatever it is, you will know by feeling it that this needs your attention.

Some might shrug and and say that it is all a 'coincidence'. Indeed it is – a *coinciding* or a coming together of energies which have provided the immediate answer to your question or present research. The amount of right intent, focus and awareness of being in the present moment will determine how successful you become at this interaction with your Higher Self and the Universe.

Getting the Connection

In a visualisation – using our imagination – we can join the Soul Star to the Earth Star with a laser-like beam which is *breathed down* through the centre of the body and through all the chakras. This is a simple way of becoming centred, as well as connecting to the Higher Self or guardian – making the Inner Column of Light. Let's have a short practice, but before you try it, put up your quick protection procedure (Rule 1).

Rule 2: Connecting Routine

Imagine your Soul Star, place of your guardian, shining above your head and its polarity, your Earth Star, pulsing brightly below your feet.

Connect your Soul Star to your Earth Star, by breathing as if your breath is coming down from the Soul Star, collecting and forming a tube of golden light passing through the top of the head (crown chakra), down through the centre of your body and connecting all the chakras, one by one, right down to the Earth Star.

There is light flowing between the two – a pathway has been re-connected. As long as you breathe *in* (as-if) through the top of your head and get down to the solar plexus area with your visualising on this in-breath, you can then focus the out-breath down through the lower chakras to the Earth Star. Do this connection three times. It doesn't matter if you make the connection with one in-breath, but in that case, you need to get rid of the out-breath still focused on the 'centre line', so breathe it out, deep down into the Earth beyond the Earth Star. This will act as a 'rooting in' device for your meditation, so nothing is lost. Do just what is comfortable for you.

At this point, you are now ready to relax the body/detox-breathing/listen to the breath or contemplate the peace. When you are ready to return, say: 'I am now closing down'. This important statement of intent instructs your whole being on many levels. I cannot emphasise it enough. When proper opening and closure procedures have been ignored, not mentioned or have been half attempted, psychic problems have been encountered and have led to many difficult disorders, both in the bodies of people and their homes. It is equivalent to going out into a blizzard in the North Pole only wearing your underclothes! It's all about looking after yourself – being responsible because you are an important package!

Rule 3: Full Closing Down Procedure
I am now closing down.

I am counting down from twelve to come back to full consciousness and will remember all my experiences.

The seal: I visualise a golden disc with an equilateral cross etched upon it being placed upon each chakra as I say the number. I start at twelve to incorporate the five chakras above my head, first focusing my attention above the head and descending onto each chakra part of the body: (slowly) ... twelve ... eleven ... ten ... nine ... eight ... seven (crown) ... six (brow) ... five (throat) ... four (heart) ... three (solar plexus) ... two (stomach/sacrum) ... one (seat/base) to the knees ... and lastly, the soles of the feet. Breathe in and breathe out, letting the breath flow down over the body to the feet and into the ground. Open the eyes ... move your feet, wriggle the toes and the hands ... stretch the arms.

Make your notes now. If you leave it, the impressions recede (as dreams often disappear). A drink and something to eat will assist the grounding – strongly advisable. As mentioned before, placing your hands under cool running water provides an excellent cleansing and closing down.

(Some experienced inner landscape travellers even jump up and down on the spot after returning, to assist the grounding of the physical body! It may sound crazy but it works well and is practical after very deep inner work.)

You notice I have introduced twelve chakras to be closed down in this full procedure. This is because the eighth chakra is the Soul Star above the crown and the others are beyond that, in the Column of Light as you activate it. This is preparation work for the changes during the next thirty years or so when many people will experience shifts in these chakras as the Column of Light or light body is built.

The full procedure is for all meditation work in this book. You can just do the shorter, countdown closure of the seven chakras for the breathing exercises.

More about Soul and Earth Stars
The Soul Star is a point of entry for the higher frequencies to enter the seventh – the crown chakra – at the top of the head. It acts as a bridge and translates and filters higher cosmic energies to the Soul level of our being. Its action on these infinite levels feeds our spiri-

tual bodies with divine inspiration, fine light particles and thus, healing, because as our own frequencies are gradually raised, a transmutation takes place.

Blockages around the crown chakra have various causes and pollute the aura. For example, when a person has overindulged in hallucinogenic drugs, has been involved in lower astral activities, has engaged in negative thinking or has negative programming (fears), the conscious activation of the Soul and Earth Stars begins a process which safely and gently begins to clear the pathway to and from the crown chakra, re-connecting the lower self to the Higher Self and infinity. For such cases, concentration on the Breath of Peace (Chapter 2) and the Breathe and Detox (Chapter 3) exercises for several weeks is recommended.

Finally, when the physical body is jettisoned (dies), the Soul enters the radiance and light of the Soul Star.

The Earth Star, positioned below the feet as the polarity to the Soul Star, funnels energy through the body to the Earth, mainly through the Inner Column of Light. The Earth Star corresponds to the soles of the feet where a smaller, secondary chakra is found in each. These form a triangle: left foot, Earth Star, right foot, which facilitates this action.

The palms of the hands also have important, secondary chakras, as mentioned previously and the excellent grounding and healing obtained by holding the hands and wrists under cold, running water after a meditation is recommended.

Guardians/guardian angels

As we have stated, the Higher Self is the primary guardian gatekeeper of the 3D space-suit working in conjunction with the Soul. The so-called guardian angels are not designated to one religious belief system, and you don't have to belong to any organisation in order to connect to them. There are writings about their presence in all religions as well as experiences constantly being recounted by folk who least suspected their existence but were helped in moments of crisis. They are particularly close to you in childhood while the Soul is being established in the physical body.

Their job description is to aid you to fulfil your destiny and to link you to the Universal Force; but they cannot interfere with your free will, so that action can only be taken by them if you request help (which initially happens when one is in dire circumstances). Be careful and specific when asking for help in other circumstances. Without proper instruction you could programme in a disfunction. For example, just asking for help with your life in general leaves the angelic beings poised for action with no direction. They do not work like a fairy godmother or genie to grant your every wish, for their energy is pure God-force energy operating with one law – love, giving and providing spiritual power when you request their help.

For the purposes of protection, you can call upon the guardian angels when going into tricky neighbourhoods, travelling, when sick, before going to sleep and so on.

The Angel of Peace is a powerful protective idea to use before or during meditations, or you can simply state which angel you require, for there is one for anything you can think of!

Some people carry or wear quartz or other crystals which enhance the body's frequencies, thus helping to create a shield from lower, negative vibrations. The use of symbols as protective devices is discussed in Chapter 7, but it should be noted that in our closing down procedure we use a gold disc with an equilateral cross on it to seal each chakra as we count down to return to full consciousness. This is a very powerful symbol of protection. The radiation of love through the heart chakra gives the most powerful protection of all, but until this has been practised, understood and nurtured, it is wise to use any or all of the other suggestions or what you feel is right for you, as progress is made.

Summary of full procedure for meditation and for going within

a   Prepare sacred space.

b   Light candle.

c   Prepare self: Settle comfortably.

d   Rule 1: Put up protection around aura and through the bodies. If desired, ask for the guardian Angel of Protection or Peace.

e   Rule 2: Connecting routine (to Higher Self – Soul Star to Earth Star).

f   Bring in the Peace with a breathing exercise.

g   The Power of Command: Relaxation routine of the physical body.

h   Move into chosen meditation.

i   Rule 3: Closing down procedure.

j   Make notes. Keep the journal.

k   Proper grounding: eat and drink.

Part Two
GETTING STARTED:
GUIDELINES FOR MIND TRAINING

5
Making contact: the way in

Every step forward opens up a new vista.

The 'way in' to anywhere is either through a gateway or a door. It is the image of a door which we will use constantly for the various guided meditations in this section.

The symbolism of the door is important to understand as a message to the mind of entering over a threshold into something new. It shows opportunity, an opening to freedom, and can be seen as moving from one state to another as you enter.

In creative meditation, it is an optimistic tool to take you into a changed experience safely and when the time comes to return, acts as a stepping-down point of exit from one level of awareness towards full consciousness when you close the door.

Everyone has, or can create, their own doorway. Sometimes you may find changes in the way it looks in its style or colour as you progress with meditating. All images are promoting your sense of awareness, for you are encouraged to look and remember what you see, for details or impressions act as useful points of reference for their meanings. Because you have linked in with your Higher Self through the Connecting Routine as part of the opening procedure, your Higher Self will begin to give you symbols as the language through which the contact between you will develop. This is why keeping a journal of your impressions immediately after the meditation is important. In time, you are likely to see a pattern of information emerging which will have a direct link to your mission in this lifetime. Of course, it will be very subtle and at first may be very random, but as you enter into more and more meditations, the symbols can become very meaningful.

The power of the imagination
Some people are said to have a vivid imagination, which is often used as a criticism against someone who has come up with an

unusual story, invention or fantasy. In creative meditation, we are calling upon our sense of imaginative creativity to take us into a protected and peaceful environment in order to promote our feeling and intuitional natures and thus to widen our concepts. We are relaxing into the experience, being guided into accomplishing mind tasks in order to gain more focus on those inner levels.

Although the imagination can go forth and multiply into pure fantasy, here we are attempting to get the mind used to operating in a safe, protected place which has been prepared to bypass fantasy and lower psychic energies. This type of introduction to meditation through visualization is helpful in gently opening the sixth (brow) chakra – or the third eye.

When you close your eyes, you will notice that they *automatically* look upwards as if to the inside of your forehead. This is where the eyes are most comfortable when closed. Open your eyes quickly and you can see an effect where the eyes have to rearrange themselves into forward focus. It may hardly be noticeable in your case at the moment, but when you have been practising meditation for a little while, you may notice it can take a little longer to re-focus the eyes on opening them, which is why a good closing down and grounding back into full consciousness is so important.

This inner screen – the inside of your forehead, as it were – is the area where the pictures can be created, intuited and inspired. The brow is both a creative and a receptive area as described in the Chakras section in Chapter 2.

In the following meditation, the physical senses of sight, touch, taste, smell and hearing are employed and used within, so that they are sharpened up as tools of experience. This exercises and develops your 'extra senses' or extra-sensory perceptions (ESP).

Read it through and try it out. As before, it may be helpful to read it slowly onto a tape so that the sequence unfolds easily without any stress of trying to remember the details. When you have completed the opening procedures to prepare for meditation, you are ready for the following mind exercise which takes place in a peaceful garden.

Exercise 5: Meditation of the Senses
In front of you is a door set in a wall. This is your own door which can lead anywhere at any time. This time we have chosen to visit a

peaceful garden. What colour is the door? What shape is it? Move closer to the door and examine it. The door has a handle. Grasp the handle, turn it and go in.

You are standing on a pathway which leads down to the bank of a stream and then runs alongside it. What is the path made of? Walk down the sloping path to the stream and a little way on, beside it, you will see a seat under a tree. Sit down on the seat and relax. It is warm and peaceful here. The sun is shining and catching the movement of the water as it runs over the stones. You can hear the sound of the bubbling water over the stones in the stream and the sound of birds singing in the tree. It is a fruit tree and you reach up to a low branch and pick a ripe fruit of your choice. You take a bite. It tastes sweet and the juice fills your mouth. It is delicious and is very refreshing. When you have finished place the remains in a litter bin next to the seat. Hear it fall into the bin.

Now get up from the seat and move to the edge of the shallow stream where there is a little beach with pebbles. Place your hand in the water and feel it run through your fingers, cool and pleasant. Now the other hand. Do they feel the same? Concentrate on how the water feels for a moment.

Among the pebbles at your feet, there is one there which attracts you. Pick it up and feel the smoothness of the pebble, look at the colour. Hold onto the pebble and make your way slowly back up the path to the door. Pause and look back at this peaceful place. Remember, it is yours and you can return at any time.

Grasp the handle of your door, open it, move through and close the door behind you. Stand upon the threshold. You have the pebble in your hand. You can feel it. Hold on to it.

You are now closing down and coming back to full consciousness, remembering all that you have experienced and feeling peaceful and calm. Starting at twelve, place the golden disc on each chakra as the number is said (slowly) ... 12 ... 11 ... 10 ... 9 ... 8 ... 7 ... 6 ... 5 ... 4 ... 3 ... 2 ... 1 ... to the knees, the feet and the Earth Star. Take some deep breaths, move feet and hands ... stretch ... and open your eyes. Without speaking, write down your impressions.

Keeping the journal

Always put down the date of your meditation in your journal. Visualise the pebble and draw and describe it as best you can. This is the article you have brought back through the levels of meditation and although it is as yet intangible, you have a quest in the next few days or weeks to *find it in tangible form*! If you say to yourself, 'Oh no, that's silly, it's not possible', you will be programming yourself into the denial of the possibility.

If you really want to journey into the power of peaceful discovery, you have to keep an open mind *on all levels*, relax, expect nothing, don't force but keep your eyes open as you go about your daily routines on the outer level of life. Here you must be prepared for any type of manifestation of the pebble and it will probably happen when you least expect it. Do you remember the points of view story and the power of observation? As you are searching primarily with your physical sight you are also activating your extra-sensory sight and in so doing, sending out your searching vibration with the law of 'like attracts like'. Eventually, something will happen to reveal your pebble to you, so don't miss it!

Having captured the image of the pebble on paper, continue to describe your journey on the inner levels, draw and describe your 'way in' – your door – its shape, size, colour and type of handle. What kind of wall was it set in? What was the pathway from the door to the stream made of/look like? What was your choice of fruit? How did it taste? The feel of the water on your right hand and then the left – were the feelings different? Did you have difficulty in visualising? How did you feel and what were your impressions? Write everything down.

The act of writing is a part of the grounding process after every meditation, so while it is not absolutely vital, it is a good discipline to undertake since the rewards of your notes will, after a while, piece together, thus developing your own inner story. As you write, you may also find that you are receiving further information or inspirations which you can understand in a logical (left-hand brain), explanatory way. This is an indication that there is a development of your ability to 'bridge the gap' between left and right brain hemispheres.

In this meditation we are establishing whether you can focus for the whole of the exercise and complete the tasks without deviating. This mind training opens up the ability to focus. We employed all of the physical senses on the inner level to draw your attention to their importance for the physical body and to realise that they have an equal importance to your other subtle bodies as sensors. Your free will then brings choices to your attention, for example, the type of fruit and choosing a pebble – a tangible image to bring back to the world of matter. The symbolism of stone (the pebble), the fruit, the pathway, the water and the tree all have very profound meanings which provide the background for your meditational journey.

If you accomplished water running over your left hand and then your right, this was tuning in to the male/female polarities of the human body. Another point associated with this is that the left hand is the 'receiving' hand and the right is the 'giving' hand. Did you find any difference between the two when meditating?

The evolving meditation

As you repeat the Meditation of the Senses, perhaps the next day, you may find the scene beyond the doorway has slightly changed. The changes happen because often, what you have experienced in the physical world is still in a state of assimilation to your outlook on life and therefore it has become a part of the *inner reflection* of your outer life.

For example, in your day-to-day life, certain events, circumstances, meetings, weather and so on, all play their part in your life's experiences which are constantly added to the sum total of yourself. This 'self', being in constant evolution second by second, is therefore always slightly different each time you bring it into meditation. It is where you bring the sum total of the knowledge of your outer senses to give you feed-back on an inner level. If you have a traumatic experience on one day and later decide to go into meditation to the peaceful place, you may notice perhaps that the stream or the pathway looks different. The place will still be peaceful – it is still a sanctuary. Any slight changes will merely be there for you to note as indicators of the present development of your perception – your awareness of yourself reacting.

The *symbolism* of what you experience on that inner level beside the stream is reflecting back information but on a very *subtle* level. It is rather like dream interpretation but comes from the more refined level of your spirituality and guidance from your Higher Self.

A dictionary of symbols will be very helpful to your understanding, for it acts as a reference. In this way, you can intellectualise or bring into your left-hand brain the experiences, feelings, patterns and colours etc. from your right-hand brain which was more enhanced through your act of meditation. (More about symbols in Chapter 7.) Do not use a book on dream interpretation for the symbols in your meditations because dreams, being from the sleep state, have a rather different frame of reference. One point to note, however, is that when you start to meditate regularly, you may notice you are dreaming more often. What is really happening is that you are remembering dreams more clearly and bringing them back to the conscious mind. You may like to record those separately in a dream journal, for all is relevant to your progress.

Control of your mind is vital to strong physical and spiritual growth.

You can only experience development through your own efforts. Reading the book is great, but putting it into practice is entirely different. Only those who have opened and maintained the lifeline to the Higher Self know what rewards lie ahead. No one can really tell you or do it for you. You can't rely on others because you are unique and their reaction, judgment and point of view is theirs. It's rather like telling someone else to eat your delicious meal in front of you and then tell you what is was like. Once you're 'hungry' enough, you won't give away that kind of 'meal' opportunity ever again. A sense of dedication to yourself and an effort to believe in and love yourself without infringing on others will quieten the mind and put you in touch with your own destiny. All growth starts from *within*.

Whatever kind of body you inhabit, with whatever genes and memories you have inherited from your ancestors, is the package you chose to serve your highest growth interests. You are stuck with it, but all the help and information you need at any point along the way you can attract to yourself in the outer world by first, going within. Like attracts like. If you allow your mind to rule with negativity – the irritating little voice which constantly tells you not to do something because ... bringing up all the excuses to persuade you out of moving forward positively, then you are letting the low frequencies of life rule. The moment the words come out, 'Look what you made me do!', a lack of responsibility for self is shown, an ability to blame others. When it is always someone else's fault or even sometimes – there is a clue that your frequency is foundering. Like attracts like.

If the inner life is balanced, the outer life will gradually rearrange itself acccordingly. It could take a while for this great truth to be realised because it is so *simple*.

Taking charge of your life is not about laying down the law to those around you and threatening all sort of things to put right what you consider to be wrong. Taking charge is deciding to concentrate on your strengths while at the same time being aware of your weaknesses. Give the strengths all you've got and love your weaknesses – have some compassion as to their origins – go into meditation mode and contemplate the matter and gain some insight into the 'greater picture' surrounding and affecting you. It is only when you are strong physically and spiritually that you can truly help others. Because of your singular effort at any time, those around you or connected to you will benefit from your increased vibrations.

This is truly beneficial to others and a great, silent service to humanity. Just remember, higher frequencies are fast and energetic, lower ones are sluggish and depressed. (Like attracts like.) Can you imagine what the world would be like if the majority lived in this way? Of course, there are times as we are learning to achieve and maintain this balance when we may feel physically and spiritually depleted. Try to close down to the outer world and open up to your inner world and breathe in peace. Ask your guardians for assistance. In Chapter 8 we will explore different ways to motivate the powers of positive thought for self-healing.

In order to develop the Meditation of the Senses further, let us settle down, go through the protection procedure and connecting routine and relax into breathing the Breath of Peace. (Remember, you will only experience development by your own efforts.) When you are ready to visit the peaceful garden, commence with the following instructions:

Exercise 6: Meditation of the Senses: the Bird
Any 'outside' noises will not disturb you.

Stand in front of your door set in the wall. Examine it first, open it and go through. Close the door behind you. You are safely in your own peaceful garden. Your feet are on the path leading down to the stream and the seat under the tree. Breathe in the fresh air and feel the warmth of the sun upon your face. As you move down the path you notice there are flowers growing beside it. Stop a moment – what colour are they? You look around and can see flowering shrubs. Move towards them. Touch the flowers on the shrubs. What type are they? Now smell their perfume.

Move towards the seat and sit down in the sun. Relax.

Now you hear a bird singing overhead – listen carefully. Let your mind focus only on the bird in the tree above you. Your mind is now on the branch of the tree with the bird. You are watching it sing. Gently move into the bird and become it. You and the bird are one. Look out of the bird's eyes. Look around the garden. Look down at the seat below. Look down at yourself sitting in the sun. Up here you are a bird singing. Why are you singing? Continue to experience the energy of the bird for a few moments. Remember everything you feel and see ...

When you are ready, move out of the bird and back onto the seat under the tree, looking out of your own eyes. Relax in the sunshine for a while and contemplate the peace. Feel it in every cell of your body, but do not go to sleep ...

This garden of peace has a small fountain of water coming out of a wall and falling into a stone basin. Get up from the seat and drink from this spring of pure water. Feel it in your mouth, cool, sweet and fresh.

It is time to go. Move towards the door along the path. Look back at the garden of peace. Remember all you have seen and experienced ... Go through the door. Close it behind you and stand upon the threshold. You are now closing down and coming back to full consciousness, feeling the peace and remembering all that you have experienced.

Starting at twelve, place the golden disc (with the etching of the equal cross upon it), as a seal on each chakra as the number is said (slowly). 12 ... 11 ... 10 ... 9 ... 8 ... 7 ... 6 ... 5 ... 4 ... 3 ... 2 ... 1 ... down to the knees, each foot and to the Earth Star. Take some deep breaths, move hands and feet ... stretch ... and open your eyes. Without speaking, write down your impressions.

Once more, this meditation can be read onto a tape very slowly as it is written because within the text there are a number of helpful key words to keep you safely on course. (Don't forget to label this tape 'Bird' to identify it.)

The development in this meditation of the senses gives you the idea of moving your consciousness into a bird, which may be new to you. This part of mind training is fascinating because it will put you in touch with all of nature, the more you practise. You can vary your target from a bird to any animal and then move into the world of trees and plants. This has the effect of expanding your 'point of view' into realising how they think or feel. There are *no limits*, only those we set in place ourselves. In this meditation, we used all of the other ideas of the different senses again with smelling the scent of flowers, feeling the warmth of the sun and drinking from the fountain of pure water which activates the intuitional, inspirational and creative self. They are very simple activities but slowly build mind strength to build the bridge between left and right brain hemispheres.

Once you have established the 'way in' – your door to the peaceful garden, grasped the outline of the map of the place in your mind and achieved the focus on the tasks to be done in the meditations, you can begin to create a wider scenario and include other things in the landscape. Bear in mind that this is your own creation of a peaceful place for yourself and no one else, which you can visit at any time. A sacred haven.

The discipline of doing the simple tasks without allowing any other thought or idea to put you off course is the test as to whether you can follow through simple creative directives to your mind in a peaceful state of consciousness.

Test yourself from your notes as to how many observations you achieved with this checklist: Door. Type of pathway. Feel the warmth of the sun on your face? Flowers beside path. Flowering shrubs – type of flowers. Smell their scent? Hear the bird singing. Did you move into the bird? Look out of its eyes? Sing as the bird? Contemplate peace? Drink from the fountain? Taste the pure water?

All of these tasks are set in a scene which you have had to imagine at the same time, so there is quite a lot to get right. The other possibility is that outside noises – perhaps a noisy motor-bike or car in the street or sounds of a radio or television near by, could act as irritants to your concentration. These sounds can take you out of alpha consciousness and need to be accepted, recognised and then ignored. (This thinking pattern takes place in an instant.) Should this happen, focus back onto your breathing and go back to where you left off. Any disturbance you experience is only a test!

6
The higher self

The power of thought is the key which holds the vision for the future

In order to work with the energies of the Higher Self, it is essential that the energy of thought be controlled and maintained.

Once again, it is one thing to read something and another to put it into practice, but your Higher Self will hear every call you make for your growth into greater understanding. Through the next meditation later in this chapter we will begin to establish our contact.

As we now know, the chakra system of the body is a major key to making good connections and unfolding the wisdom you require for life's journey. As we saw in Chapter 2, the seven chakras of the body are comprised of the first three chakras: base, sacral and solar plexus, called the lower chakras. The upper chakras of throat, brow and crown form the higher chakras, while the heart is the central, mediating chakra, which is the key to connecting with the Higher Self.

The pure energy of the heart is love and compassion.

The heart is the centre of all wisdom for it is the place where the subconscious mind connects to the Divine.

A lot of people are locked into the energies of the lower three chakras for a variety of reasons but mainly because of the learning involved in survival skills through the early years of life, which have become so habitual in a material-based world that nothing better is considered.

Gradually, over time, this habit is so established that the other four chakras are sometimes barely operating as a result of the lack of awareness that there is a greater picture. This state of affairs can continue throughout adulthood, so there can be a lack of developed sensitivity, compassion and a disregard for anyone else but the lower self. We call this a lifestyle that is operating with the lower ego, where the baser instincts are in command of the physical vehicle.

In total contrast, there are others who have developed the higher chakras and the lower ones are just ticking over. This can lead to a difficulty in grounding the finer frequencies and the person can become detached from the physical world. Perhaps the majority of people are in various 'in between' stages. Once there is a conscious decision for growth, enquiry and seeking, we are opening up to our metaphysical self and thus beginning the adventure of alignment to the Cosmos. The task is to learn how to bring about *inner* balance and harmony which in turn is expressed outwardly, because everything starts from within.

Every chakra has a different part in upholding the health of all the bodies (the physical, the subtle and the spiritual bodies), so a balanced and gradual approach is vital. This is why our connecting routine, breathing through the top of the head down to the feet, is so important to establish from the beginning. It builds gradually over time, into a pillar of light energy connecting the chakras and bringing in more of the Higher Self to operate from the heart. Of course, this is accomplished by intent, will and action.

More about the ego

The Higher Self (the Permanent Self), is an individual spark of the Source or God Force which connects you to all things and the Soul works in conjunction with it. What we call the ego is a structure which links to the senses. It processes information from the senses through the action of the brain to focus it into third-dimensional understanding. The ego is the communication device for the Soul in the physical world, so you can see the Higher Self has this extension as part of the evolutionary structure for the Soul, so that it has feedback about the current state of the physical life. The programming of the subconscious is part of the ego function. If we can understand that by bringing this ego into the heart, the centre for all wisdom, to conjoin with the Higher Self, we can become fully realised into our primary mission or Soul Path. An enlightenment takes place when all the chakras are clear, aligned and can form the Column of Light.

'Ego' is Latin for 'I am'. It acts as your anchor in the third dimension which is needed to organise your physical world. It also acts out of love for its self-preservation.

Nowadays we understand 'ego' as a word to describe selfish, egotistical or self-centred. For example, some people work on a silent manipulation of others and imply that 'if you don't do this for me you are selfish', trying to make you feel guilty. If you allow anyone to manipulate you in this kind of way, they are really disempowering you. The word 'egotistical' is in alignment with the negative and 'ego' with the positive. This indicates how a once perfectly good structure has been split apart by the constant lowering of the human vibration into material denseness until we now only recognise the word 'ego' as negative. We should realise that ego was really designed to function as a perfect tool of self-empowerment communicating with love for the Self and the Higher Self/Soul to bring about a creative and joyous physical existence where there is an absence of fear. Love is the absence of fear. You can see how distorted everything has become in humanity's race for materialistic evolution.

Soul-self versus Ego-self

When you are coming from the heart and you know you are, with deep, core, gut feeling and instinct, then you are acting out of your Soul-Self. The 'negative' ego operating for survival will construct, devise, rewrite scenarios and develop courses of conduct for self-preservation at any (one's) cost. This type of negative action can be brought into harmony and the hidden agendas recognised by telling the ego that you are observing why the conduct has been negative and that you are going to love this part of the ego free. In other words, you are re-programming your subconscious self and letting go of fears.

'Love is letting go of fear' is a saying with deep meaning. This is the love called unconditional love, meaning a love without any conditions attached, unlike 'I'll love you if you love me' type of negotiation. Unconditional loving is from deep compassion and honour.

To act truly out of the higher ego does not mean doing great works to the detriment of one's own body health, for this is martyrdom, nor do you need to sacrifice your very Soul Self. The real responsibility lies firstly in honouring, loving and caring for this physical vehicle which you have created – growing it and feeding it and keeping it in good condition in order to experience many adventures from which to learn. Secondly, in giving your service, your help and love to others freely (without conditions) and expecting nothing in return.

By perfecting communication with all of your divine essence – your Higher Self, you can ask for help in loving every part of yourself, especially any parts which make you feel uncomfortable.

In this way, you will become free from guilt, fear, manipulation and control which is the key to peace and harmony within. Sometimes, you may have to let go of people who are not in harmony with you anymore. Healing constantly takes place as we recognise the nuances behind our own actions and reactions and resolve to let go and love them free. Loss of the lower ego is not loss of individuality or loss of power, it is the gaining of your true identity, true self and is the gaining of power over lower, negative impulses and restrictions to a better existence where we are able to love others as we would wish to be loved ourselves. Only then, will 'harmonious like' truly attract 'harmonious like'. The true Ego or 'I am' presence of your being, then becomes the perfect communicator of self-acceptance and self-love in the physical world, which is what it was always meant to be. Love is the knowing and accepting of oneself.

The heart is the 'temple', or sacred space in your 3D spacesuit for the Soul-Self. It is the meeting place where discernment and mediation takes place between all of your many parts of 'self' and where lies freedom.

Now let us start to make the connections to the heart and the Higher Self by bringing everything into action through a meditation.

Exercise 7: Temple of the Heart Meditation

Read through the meditation first and, if you wish, tape it for your own use, speaking slowly. Prepare and settle down in your space, close your eyes and complete the protection, breathing and relaxation procedures. Outside noises will not disturb you.

In front of you is your door. As you look at the door, call upon your guardians to be with you now. Grasp the handle of the door and open it. Move over the threshold and close the door behind you.

You are standing on a path of golden light which leads to a beautiful white building in front of you. It is your Temple of the Heart. You can already feel the peace rising from the temple and encircling you (pause to experience).

Let this loving energy move you forward towards the white marble steps leading up to the door. Go up the steps and pause at the door. Look at it and remember its shape and colour. Grasp the handle and move inside, closing the door behind you.

You are in a beautiful, circular courtyard with a floor of smooth shining emerald. In the centre of the courtyard is a fountain of water falling into a pool with pink and cream lilies floating on its surface. The air is full of delicate perfume. Breathe it in (pause). Beyond the courtyard is a rose garden. Move towards it. There are columns of white and pink marble and archways upon which the roses climb in profusion. Luxurious green ferns grow in between. Walk under the archways of roses and ferns (pause). Walk around this beautiful place and find an arbour with seats where you can relax in the warm sunshine and enjoy the surroundings (pause).

Sit and breathe in the white, pink and green atmosphere into your heart chakra, then let it flood your whole body, into every cell and through all the subtle bodies. Let the emerald floor absorb any negative, lower vibrations coming out through your hands and feet as you clear them. Concentrate on this task for a few moments (pause). Now it is time to call your Higher Self into this place – your Temple of the Heart. With your breath coming in from above your head through the Soul Star, silently speak your request:

'Come Higher Self, divine part of me, into my heart temple which I have now prepared.' Repeat this three times. Wait ... When you feel the presence of your Higher Self enter the arbour, note the signal you receive in or on your body. It may be a tingle, shiver, sound – anything – but try to establish it. Ask for an impression of the form of your Higher Self. Relax the body but remain alert in the mind and wait (pause). Be still ... seek the stillness ... be at peace ... let the peace and the love embrace you (long pause – give yourself at least one minute of silence here).

You will remember everything you have experienced (pause). It is time to leave. Move through the temple to the main door, pass through it and close it behind you. Walk down the steps along the golden pathway to your own personal door. Pause a moment. Hanging on a hook beside the door is a long, dark cloak with a hood. Put it on, pulling the hood over your head. Feel the warmth of the cloak as you wrap it around yourself. Remember the colour of the cloak. Now open the door, pass over the threshold and close the door behind you.

You are now closing down, allowing the Higher Self to shift back into the correct level for you at this time and coming back to full consciousness, remembering all that you have experienced, bringing the love, peace and serenity with you. Starting at twelve, place the golden disc to seal each chakra as the number is said (slowly). 12 ...

11 ... 10 ... 9 ... 8 ... 7 ... 6 ... 5 ... 4 ... 3 ... 2 ... 1 ... to the knees, the feet and the Earth Star. Take some deep breaths, move your hands and feet ... open your eyes and stretch ... Silently thank your guardians and Higher Self for their contact and assistance.

Without speaking, write down and draw all your impressions.

Try to do this meditation at least once a week after you have mastered the opening and closing procedures with relaxation and purposeful breathing plus the previous meditations.

If you are new to meditating, it is important to lead up to this one gradually, with a little bit of practice under your belt before you attempt it. Not that it's difficult, but you need to feel ready to take on the responsibility of this more conscious Higher Self contact. Enjoy the early limbering up procedures and meditations for those exercises are not only beneficial for re-programming the mind, but also benefit your health. The time you give to yourself in this way also gradually builds spiritual muscle.

In this Temple of the Heart meditation, you will notice some new, important tasks to accomplish. Your extra sensory perceptions are being widened to encompass finer energies on higher levels.

You will notice that your guardians are asked to accompany you and at the end of the meditation, you thank them and your Higher Self. This is *very important* for it is correct protocol which should be programmed into your spiritual nature. Don't take anything for granted. Guardians are assigned to you from birth and are usually closely connected to you from other lifetimes such as from your own past family background or beings who work on the angelic frequencies in service to humanity.

True guides or guardians will not interfere or impose upon you, for your free will is sacred, so if you need guidance, protection or assistance in an activity, you always have to ask for it. (Earlier, we mentioned the angels working in the same way.) Help will never be denied you, although it can take many unusual forms in the outer world. If you are in danger and it's not yet your time for transition, your guardians will arrange beneficial influences with your Higher Self for your highest possible good. In creating this Heart Temple you are preparing a meeting place between you, the personality and the key factor in the Power of Peace within you, which is love.

The meeting between you and your Higher Self takes place even if you don't specifically recognise it at first, for it is so subtle. The feeling of 'presence' will certainly unfold, whatever your background in religion, cultural traditions or belief systems. The love that your Higher Self has for you is totally without conditions and cannot interfere with this. It holds an overview of your life and will endeavour to help you to evolve into something greater by providing opportunities for growth. It will make no demands, will not control, is the best loving companion you could wish for and is able to convey the most terrific sense of joy in your everyday life. Allow that loving energy into every cell of your body for you have made contact with your divinity and inner teacher – the higher aspect of yourself.

The symbolism of all the factors in this temple are profound and pure. The whole scenario is meaningful from the architecture and materials used, to the geometry or shapes seen and the colours, flowers, scent and atmosphere.

Once again, a dictionary of symbols will help you to understand this secret language and as mentioned previously, it is this language which your guardians and Higher Self will use most often to communicate knowledge to you. More about symbolism in Chapter 7.

The visualisation provided in this meditation is a guideline to give you an idea of creating a 'way in' to the love of the heart.

When you succeed in feeling the presence of your Higher Self in the rose garden arbour and have received the code of recognition as some kind of feeling in your physical body, you will find this most helpful in outer life when you ask for assistance and get this personal response. That will convince you if nothing else that your Higher Self is a fact of life!

Once this is established, you may like to ask for a name which identifies your Higher Self. Ask for this to be written up for you on your inner screen or spoken to your extra-sensory hearing if you have found sounds to be more enhanced in your understanding. You will also notice in this meditation: *Ask for an impression of the form of your Higher Self.* Did you get anything?

Perhaps you saw a colour or colours, a shape or a 'being' in human form, or was it an impression or feeling that gave you an idea of form? Whatever it was, check this out next time you do this meditation and establish this form of your Higher Self on the inner planes. Don't worry if you didn't receive an impression of form. It is more unusual than usual to have a clear visual picture of your Higher Self, especially in the early stages of communication.

Lastly in this meditation, there was a dark cloak waiting for you just before you passed through your own doorway. This serves two purposes: firstly, to act as a closing down device for your aura which steps down the vibration for returning to base. It will also protect you. Secondly, the colour, although dark, may or may not be significant to your present conditions or circumstances, which is why you are requested to remember it. Think of chakra colours and/or the meaning of colours. For example, if the cloak was brown, it is a good grounding colour and its composition is really made up from a mixture of several colours. There is *nothing* sinister in your choice of colour. View everything you experience as positive and helpful to your unfoldment.

From now on, it is wise to keep silent about the particular codes of recognition that you have established between you and your Higher Self, especially if you are working in a group and have discussions after meditations. Anything else may be shared and you will learn much from each other's experiences.

How can you tell what is truth and what is delusion? How can you tell whether the inner voice you are hearing is *really* your Higher Self? Is all this meditation stuff an imaginative joke?

These are the type of questions most often posed by people who don't meditate or who haven't taken the trouble to inform themselves about the many subjects available for metaphysical study – and most of all they are displaying some hidden fear. You can also get this type of challenge from the 'joker' who wants to score some points off you. All of this is natural in today's varied society. Nevertheless, they are certainly valid questions requiring answers or reminders about what we have explored thus far.

In order to test the validity of the information and impressions you have gained through creative meditating, *bring them into the heart*. You can go on and on thinking about something, but if you *feel* through the heart, you will always find your truth. In the same way, if somebody tells you something which may sound amazing at first – take it to your heart – how does it feel now? Employ your feeling processes to find what is truth. Your mental processes will organise strategy. If you come across information that doesn't feel right for you in that moment, this does not necessarily mean that it isn't truth. It can mean that yes, it isn't right for you at this present time. Your *discernment* is being tested! There is a lot of misinformation and disinformation about, but there is also an enormous amount of good, sound knowledge available, some of which has been handed down through the ages and some breaking through new boundaries.

Your Higher Self – your divine spark and inner teacher – will welcome your challenges which can take the form of questions asking for proof of identity, proof of validity etc.

Don't be 'half-hearted' in your approach to questions or being open to receive answers.

If that is what you want – then prepare the place for the dialogue – that is, yourself moving into the Temple of the Heart, and before you commence your meditation, write down your questions so that you are clear about them. The best teacher for you – is you – the Higher Self part of you or as some may prefer to call it, the divine spark of God that you are. That spark will do its best to help you for, as it is part of the Source it can refer to the Source at all times (as can you).

When you are more familiar with the feeling of the Higher Self presence within, events and circumstances that occur in daily life will be viewed in a different way. For example, anyone feeling they have been or are a 'victim' of circumstance will begin to realise that there is a greater picture to be considered. Yes, it is tough at times but this is a planet of learning and that is why we all chose to be here at this time. We are not alone.

The Power of Love

If we are here in a body, we are loved by the Creator because all is created by love. Denying ourselves the ability to contact our divine essence is a denial of our very creation. The only barriers to making this contact are in ourselves – our attitude and lack of love, faith and trust. The Power of Love is an energy which moves and performs in action. We exist because of love and because love is the creative force of the Universe.

The true identity of love is often distorted, misplaced or solely interpreted through the physical channel of our emotional body.

The sexual energy with which we are all gifted can be mistaken for the true essence of love, although of course, it can be our expression of love.

We will continue to attract and take part in emotional dramas as long as we need to learn about the different shades of love manifesting in the physical world.

The possessive energy in relationships accompanied by bargaining and manipulative power can be identified as a distortion of love. These ideas and many others are often formed in early life through the experiences a child or young person has in their particular environment.

Later on in the adult world, the stress, demands and laws of society can promote other survival techniques which can leave little time, room or inclination to develop an understanding of love. Consequently, people can get stuck in the lower chakras, as we have mentioned before, with the result that the heart energy is hardly touched – until one day, there is a personal, traumatic event which will trigger off feelings held deep inside. Possible confusion and trauma are the result.

The true, unconditional nature of love, that is, love which has no conditions attached to it at all, is what we are always seeking and it is hidden in the heart:

The key to understanding the power of love is – forgiveness.

When we are ready to forgive from the heart and let go – then we know the true power of love.

The power of unconditional love in action will promote all other powers to manifest for the highest possible good.

7

The power of symbols, signs and patterns

Man's evolution unfolds when hidden language can be translated and understood

In the previous chapter we have hopefully made some kind of contact with the Higher Self through the meditation in the Temple of the Heart, albeit perhaps a tentative one. It will take some practice to feel changes, but do remember we are dealing with *subtle*, higher frequency energies. Your sincere intent, without forcing yourself in any way, is enough to unite you with who you truly are, and from then on, provided you keep up the link in both a conscious and meditative way, will all be fine tuning. By conscious, I mean being aware that the Higher Self influence is always within you (always has been) and comes through into your waking, daily life activated by thought. If you have been attempting to tune in through all the previous exercises and meditations, you should have some information in your notebooks about the observations you have made along the way thus far – your personal experience. Some experiences occur during meditation which at the time make no sense to the conscious mind, for you may have observed a language of geometric shapes, patterns, colours and strange scenes that you didn't expect.

Don't forget, the right-hand hemisphere of the brain, and your intuitive mind, is receiving information and your left-hand logical hemisphere is trying to find files which can bring some sense to these observations. It can all be dismissed so easily as having a dreamlike or even a nonsense quality – but wait. This is where the hidden language begins to help you bridge the gap.

Symbols can be interpreted in many ways. There is the obvious, straightforward interpretation with which our conscious mind has already been trained to recognise and identify, through explanations coming from diverse cultures and religions.

Then there are psychological interpretations, dream analysis and sacred geometry. All these views are not really separate one from another, but overlap and interpenetrate each other, depending on which emphasis is pursued.

In creative meditation, we must be careful to observe that symbols can have both an exoteric – an outer, worldly meaning – and esoteric – an inner, spiritual, hidden meaning. Symbolism can be effective on more than one level at the same time, but its effectiveness will be restricted only to the degree that it is understood. In other words, it will depend on how well our intelligence and spirituality can interpret, research it and ultimately, get some understanding in both a mental and feeling (emotional) way from it. This is why you are encouraged to write down everything immediately after your meditation so that you can contemplate and interpret your impressions for yourself. We are entering a landscape in meditation as both an observer and a partaker. In the beginning we hope to *receive* something – the 'what's in it for me' syndrome, but gradually, as we develop, we are both receiving and giving ourselves to the Power of Peace where opinion, judgment and restriction are set aside to allow a unity with the Cosmos to occur within ourselves. We build trust.

One symbol, sign or pattern can represent a wealth of information, for it is the language of pictures which trigger words which give meaning. It doesn't matter what language you speak daily, the symbolic representations bypass that. Eventually, you develop a state of just 'knowing' – which is beyond words. Examples are everywhere from national flags, company logos, heraldry, planetary symbols, shorthand, morse code, secret codes, road signs, astrological signs, mathematics and chemical formulas, to name but a few.

Many of these we learn because we have to know them for our working roles, others for our leisure interests and others we are aware of but don't employ at all.

If we take secret codes from the above list, we are looking at the science of cryptology (from the Greek *kryptos*, meaning hidden, and *logos*, word) which deals with creating and deciphering secret messages much developed and employed during the Second World War and from where the modern computer has its roots.

Ancient Egyptian hieroglyphics demonstrate the use of inscribed information on both public buildings and inscriptions within the temples, which were only for the eyes of the priests, priestesses and the initiated. Gradually, the last-mentioned invented and changed texts and ritual instruction so that it became even more secret or hidden.

One of the greatest hidden codes of all time has been the RNA/DNA stranded codes of the human body, the discovery of which has now opened up all kinds of amazing information from our inherited genetics.

The secrets of the human mind and activities of the brain are continuing to be fathomed. One demonstration of this in the latter part of the twentieth century was the intense training of people in various countries to undertake mind tasks in order to infiltrate secret or military zones, using the technique called Remote Viewing. This has also been used to locate missing persons, investigate crimes and uncover evidence regarding supernatural events.

Another is the use of therapies which uncover the experiences of people having what seem to be other lives which they are able to relive. To the observer, it can mean little. To the person reliving the experience it is often an amazing breakthrough which brings sense to their current lifetime. You can understand denials by people of many of these kinds of possibilities when they are not informed.

Mind-expanding techniques in one form or another develop extra-sensory awareness to give a greater perception of the world and the energies at play which are normally hidden from ordinary sight and experience.

In all these areas, it would seem that right intent and integrity are very desirable. Taking into account that there is some lack of this in our society today is one of the reasons why we have a code of practice in this book for the protection of your third-dimensional spacesuit. I have noticed a lot of people say how wonderful it would be to become invisible, but when asked how they would feel about others 'spying' on them, then a rethink occurs!

For our purposes, we are looking at a symbol in two ways: as having an obvious meaning (which is only half the story), and with hidden meanings which can stem from a variety of ancient sources to illumine and bring about its completion. This idea satisfies the emotions, intellect and the higher, spiritual nature.

For example, in Chapter 5 there was an introduction to the 'way in' by creating a door – your door – for the Meditation of the Senses. This entrance acts as a movement from one level to another – from one world into another – entering into a new life. Visualising a door and, later, describing it should give you an idea of your present way of thinking and what is happening with you in your life right now. Is

83

your door in good condition? Is it partly hidden by creepers or undergrowth – a secret entrance?

If you saw ivy hanging over it, then that can symbolise immortality, eternal life or a clinging attachment or dependence shrouding the entrance. If you identify with the latter in your life, then smile in acceptance and shift your perspective to another, positive meaning to ivy which includes constancy in affection and friendship. Choose the best for yourself, but note carefully what came up in the first instance and when you next meditate and ask for your door, note if any changes have occurred.

I have noticed that people often start off with a solid oak door, perhaps a gothic style with studs on it and wrought iron tracery – and why not? A bit of drama sets the stage for a grand entrance. If the word 'oak' comes into your description, then once again, we have the meaning of strength, truth and sacredness to add to the picture of your 'way in'.

In the Temple of the Heart meditation, I suggested that after you had entered through your own door, you should go along a golden pathway up the white, marble steps to the temple door and remember what it looked like before entering. This doorway is a second shift to help move you into a higher frequency. The scene was set or prepared as you went along with visualisation to help you to achieve it. What was that door like, or didn't you get that far this time? Don't worry. This is quite normal. Write down how you felt about the idea. Perhaps the word temple bothers you. (When returning, we always retrace our steps in order to step down our energy field and get back to the lower resonances of the physical world.)

You can see how so much information is staring us in the face on all levels of this life's journey if we would only give ourselves time to be still, look, listen and observe. Your Higher Self is brilliant at the game of placing symbols in your path, so be on the look-out.

Don't forget, however, that you need to establish a relationship first, in order to tap into the higher wisdom and metaphysical meanings of symbols and signs. A long time ago, I kept seeing astrological signs and symbols in my meditations and recorded them in my notebook. As a result, I began to study astrology and learned their meanings with the patterns and movements of the planets, Sun and Moon. A whole new world of understanding opened up to me, far more complex and meaningful than newspaper 'star signs'.

Tarot cards are another set of powerful symbols which are often misunderstood, perhaps because the early versions seemed to have such strange pictures and were associated with some kind of dangerous, hocus-pocus activity and fortune telling. In more recent times, with an understanding of hidden knowledge, tarot cards are becoming the tool for which they were originally intended, as an aid to self knowledge and higher wisdom, for they are representing, in picture and number, some profound symbolism. Everything has its place and serves a purpose, but never let it stop there. Look for the hidden factors and the higher levels of information just waiting to be tapped.

In this book you can see how we are using visualisation as a tool, initially, to open up to a higher level frequency to access the hidden, inner landscapes within ourselves, where knowledge can begin to flow through from higher levels of wisdom.

It is as if a stage has been set with the door opening onto a suggested landscape and the film is rolling with you as both the observer and the player. In the beginning you carry out practice tasks in this symbolic place, which slowly acclimatises your mind to different possibilities, and then you gradually build bridges of understanding with any symbols that are shown to you or which you experience in the landscape.

These will often be active and moving, not flat, two-dimensional graphics that we see on a paper. Holographic experiences, where you become part of the symbol or pattern, are common. You can also observe, remain still and watch the movements unfold. No longer are you restricted from your 'point of view' like the people in the Art Class back in Chapter 2. You can move in any direction around an object or become part of it as you did with the bird in the tree looking out of its eyes. Every time you meditate and hold your focus, you add a little more to your development. Theory is helpful but the practice and focus of meditation is the only way really to *know*.

The following examples of symbols can have as many as seven levels of understanding. This selection is provided only for your quick reference after meditation and is not intended to be learned or memorised.

An A–Z mini-reference of symbols

Alpha   Greek sign for the first letter of the alphabet 'A'. Signifies 'the beginning', with the Greek Omega as 'the end' of all things.

These letters often appear on architecture.

Animals Linked to the instinctive and intuitive nature of man. Different types link with the four elements (e.g. bird with air). Can be powerful aids and guardians in meditations. One of the four kingdoms of the world (animal, human, plant and mineral).

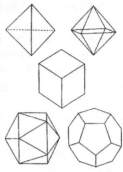

Ankh Egyptian symbol of life and immortality incorporating both male and female principles. A symbol like a key connecting one to hidden, ancient wisdom. Meditation on this symbol will provide further information.

Examples of sacred geometry: platonic solids for visualisation

Apple Knowledge, joy, fertility. Fruit of the Tree of Life. Apple tree associated with health and immortality. Apple blossom is a Chinese symbol of peace and beauty.

Aquarius Eleventh sign of the Zodiac. Associated with the New Age and the millennium. An air sign. The wavy lines of the symbol denote electricity passing through the ether or it can be read as air waves. The picture of a person – the Water-bearer – denotes man who is pouring water from a vessel, symbolic as the *water of consciousness* being shared. Communications of all kinds, satellite, TV, radio, telephone, telepathy (ESP) are connected with this sign.

Bee Messengers between worlds: 'Telling the bees' of an important event is a tradition linked with this. Immortality, Soul, rebirth. Wisdom. Order and industry. Appears in many ancient myths and different religions as wise and beneficent.

Bird Soul, spirit, good auspices. Ability to communicate with the 'gods' or attain a higher state of consciousness. Imagination, thought. Associated with tree symbolism as divine power descending into the Tree of Life. Feathers and wearing feathers symbolise spiritual journeying.

Book The Universe. Open book: book of Life, Wisdom and Knowledge. Seeking and searching as the pages are turned.

Bridge The crossing between this world and the next. The passage from the 'unreal' to the 'real'. Gaining higher states of consciousness. Associated with the rainbow as a bridge between worlds.

Butterfly The Soul, immortality. The caterpillar represents the physical world which through its dissolution is reborn into the butterfly, symbolising transformation and resurrection.

Cave The Universe. The centre, associated with the heart. A place of union between the ego and the self. Place of initiation and of mystery, healing and rebirth/renewal.

Circle Wholeness and totality. Contained, infinite, without beginning or end – timeless eternity. Time enclosing space. All cyclic movement. A circle with a dot in the centre denotes a perfect cycle and the astrological symbol for the Sun.

Cloak Symbol of both protection and dignity. Concealment, mystery. Denotes taking on a role – transforming from one purpose to another.

Colours Active colours are red, orange and yellow which return light. Passive are those which absorb light: blue and violet. Green is produced by a mix of 'active' yellow with 'passive' blue. (Identify this explanation with the chakra colours.) Black and white represent negative and positive.

Cross Universal symbol from remote, ancient origins. The vertical line is the celestial/spiritual, positive, active, male. The horizontal line is earthly, rational, passive, female. The construction shows dualism, union of opposites, spiritual union. Denotes spiritual expansion in all four directions coming from the sacred centre. (There is a wealth of symbolism here to research, coming from all cultures and religions.)

Crystal The state of clarity, self luminous, spiritual perfection. Glass (crystal) towers, bridges and glass slippers (like Cinderella's), show the transfer from material form to a finer, pure, transparent plane.

Dog Guardian, loyalty, friendship. Watches over the boundaries between worlds.

Dolphin King of fish. Power of the oceans, healers by sound, teachers to mankind. Guide to Souls, especially through transition processes. Said to be masters of the ancient, lost Atlantis, embodied as dolphins together with whales.

Dove Sacred spirit of life and light. Purity, simplicity. Messenger of peace (holding olive branch) and the renewal of life (goddess Athene). Depicts feminine principle: mother, caring, protecting. Emblem of the Knights of the Grail. White dove: purified Soul.

Eagle Sky god. Represents Air element. Denotes spiritual victory, strength and authority with ability to fly heavenwards. Identified with the Sun – the solar principle.

Earth Great/Earth Mother. Matter. Archetype of creativity and sustenance. Northern hemisphere corresponds to Yang, positive, southern hemisphere to Yin, negative.

East Spring, sunrise, dawn. New life/new beginnings. First of the four cardinal directions. Mostly associated with the Fire element. Concerned with spiritual principles of enlightenment and illumination. Revered in religious and belief systems.

Elements Fire, water, earth and air. The four passive forces of nature for western civilisations. *Fire:* upward-pointing triangle. *Water:* downward-pointing triangle. *Earth:* square or cube or downward-pointing triangle with bar across centre. *Air:* Circle or arc, or upward-pointing triangle with bar across centre. There are five elements in Taoism: wood, earth, water, fire and metal and, in Hinduism and Buddhism, earth, water, fire, air and ether.

Eye The all-seeing divinity. Symbol of all Sun-gods. The eye (or 'I') of the mind. Illumination, knowledge, protection. Egyptian: the eye of Horus; the right eye is the Sun Ra, Osiris, the left eye, the Moon, Isis. An eye in the centre of a triangle is the 'all-seeing eye' – ever-present. The third eye/brow chakra: vision, intuition. Seen as the eye of the heart: spiritual presence, illumination.

Fire/flame Symbol of consciousness for the Higher Self. Illumination, transformation, regeneration, purification, transmutation, protection. Associated with the Sun as life and light.

Flower Creative, feminine principle. As a bud it shows potential. In opening it shows development coming into manifestation – a flowering. Children, purity. Sustaining and strengthening to the emotions. Can indicate a time of year. e.g. daffodils – spring. Research the meanings of various flowers for they can be very significant.

Foot/feet/footprints Travelling life's road. Grounding, being in the moment. Support, humility. Leaving a mark of presence.

Fountain Eternal life, immortality. Water of life. In a setting like a garden or courtyard it denotes a 'centre' from which flows all life-giving forces. In the act of drinking, one partakes of knowledge – grace is given.

Garden The peaceful place or mystic journey of the Soul, paradise. Enclosed gardens show the femine principle of protection – place of the goddess. Roses growing signify eternal spring.

Gate (threshold) Associated with wisdom. Entrance to new life. Passing through/over into another dimension, opening and entering into communication. Meeting point, usually guarded by symbolic animals: lions, dogs.

Gold Symbol of the Sun. Rays or showers of gold denote gifts of spiritual wisdom, illumination, protection, perfection, sacred quality.

Grail As a cup/vessel is said to contain a perpetual supply for every need. Abundance, rejuvenation, immortality. Associated with the heart centre as the container of life. A pond/pool containing water is symbolic of a grail or chalice.

Grapes Wisdom, hospitality. Symbolises the growth, fertility leading to immortality.

Hand Expression of power, strength, blessing, peace, friendship, pledge, union, healing, welcome, prayer. The right hand is the hand of power, the left is receptive. (Numerous other symbols from religions and ancient cultures.)

Head With the heart, the two prime parts of the body. Denotes wisdom, control, life-force, seat of the Soul. Nodding to another, pledges the life-force. Bowing is to honour/show respect. Two heads together, show past/future, cause/effect. Three heads show past/present/future. Heads on fountains: refreshment, power of speech.

Heart The centre of physicality and spirituality. Compassion, love. Temple of God, mystic centre or divine centre. Symbolised by the lotus, lily or rose.

Horns Denotes the power of life or Soul arising from the head. Strength, victory, protection. Attributed to all mother goddesses. Horned gods are lords of the Animal kingdom as Pan the god of nature. Pluto, a god of abundance and wealth has a horn of plenty, (cornucopia).

Incense Associated with the element air. The smoke rising suggests prayers ascending from the below (earth) to the above (heaven). Purification, protection. Perfume of virtue, bestows immortality to departing Souls.

Island Mystical isolation, retreat, safety and refuge (being surrounded by water gives protection). A spiritual place of the blessed.

Jester/fool Ignorance, playfulness, diversion. Can indicate foolishness, choices to be made; the lower, physical self on the spiritual journey. Holds both male/female principles (opposite to king, which symbolises supremacy – an all-powerful being).

Jewels Hidden treasures of knowledge and truth. The fashioning of gems/stones indicates the honing of the Soul ultimately to reflect divine light. Wisdom. All stones have properties used in healing and symbolism, e.g. Emerald: immortality. Clarity of understanding, hope.

Key Powers of opening and closing. Giving access, securing. Gold keys to unlock spiritual power. Silver: earthly power. A gift of responsibility.

Knight Represents the quest of the spiritual journey – the initiate. When mounted on a horse (matter) it shows surmounting the material world in order to master the spirit. A guardian of the body, sacred places and brotherhoods to uphold justice and truth.

Labyrinth A path of unfolding, testing and attainment: the way of the initiate. A mysterious movement leading towards the 'centre' and returning. To find one's way in trust. Depicted in carvings, on the ground and in dance. Protection. Very ancient, complex symbol with many levels of meaning.

Light Blessing of divine manifestation. Information, illumination, revelation, direct knowledge (en-lightenment), ultimate reality. The light of the Sun (fire), is direct knowledge and of the Moon, indirect or reflected from others.

Lion Solar and lunar, yet of the fiery principle with courage, fortitude, strength and justice. Protector. Lions' heads as waterspouts show the merging of fire (lion/Sun) and water to benefit the earth. The lioness as a maternal symbol is associated with the Great Mother and many goddesses of the ancient worlds.

Lotus Called the Flower of Light and of sacred, ancient origins. Said to be the first flower – the result of the action of the fire (Sun) upon the waters. A union of the dualistic forces of Sun and Moon. Opens with the Sun and closes at sunset. It bears buds, seeds and flowers all at the same time, so represents past, present and future, symbolic of creation and the wheel of life. Purity, perfection, beauty, health, peace, harmony.

Mirror The Soul. Self-realisation, reflected wisdom and truth. Magical window.

Moon The eye of night. Mostly seen as a femine power. Depicts the rhythm and cycles of time, from new Moon (new beginnings/ideas) to full Moon (manifestation and fulfilment), as also through its control of tides, waters and seasons. The personality.

Mountain The meeting place in the clouds, of heaven and earth – hence mountains are sacred places on earth. Mountain tops are said to be the state of full consciousness. Eternity, attainment, solidity, stillness.

Numbers In Pythagorean, Hindu and Babylonian traditions, the objective world, the harmony of the Universe and the origin of everything proceeds from number. Not merely a state of quantity, but also of symbolic quality. Each number has significance in knowledge and understanding from one – the beginning, the creator, developing through to number nine – completion. Ten, the decad, holds all numbers, symbolising divinity, the Cosmos, the perfect number returning to unity, (one plus nought=ten).

Oak The human body. Strength, courage, protection. Sacred tree to Druids, American Indians, Zeus/Jupiter and Thor. Often represents lightning and fire.

Ocean Source of all life containing all possibilities/potential.

Olive The branch is a symbol of peace – also shown with the dove as peace. The leaf denotes renewal of life. Immortality, fertility, achievement – hence a crown of wild olives for the victor in the Olympic games.

Palm A Tree of Life – self-creative. Symbolises victory, triumph and blessings.

Paradise An enclosed garden or sacred space, an island, place for the resting of the Soul, where time stands still.

Peacock Love, longevity, royalty. Emblem of the Ming dynasty. In the feather, the eye is associated with the 'eye of the heart'. (Many other cultural traditions.)

Pearl Life-giving power of the Great Mother. Birth, rebirth and fertility. Innocence, perfection and humility. The 'pearl of great price' is attaining enlightenment and wisdom. Arising out of the waters, Aphrodite/Venus is the 'lady of the pearls'.

Phoenix Death by fire, rebirth and resurrection, symbolising immortality. The 'fire bird', royal, unique and noble.

Queen Great Mother or Queen of Heaven with a crown of stars. Signifies feminine command over the heavens, stars and Moon. Blue and silver.

Rainbow Each colour represents different states of consciousness. The symbolic meeting of heaven and earth. A bridge. An agreement.

River River of life is the macrocosm, river of death the microcosm. Rivers symbolise creative power coming from a hidden source. At the mouth where it joins with the ocean is the gateway to unity – all drops unite into the one ocean. Enlightenment is tracing the river back to its 'source'.

Rose Twofold symbol of heavenly perfection and earthly passion. The rose garden is a symbol of paradise where a 'union of opposites' takes place. Depicts secrecy, discretion – hung in the ceilings of council chambers (sub rosa). In heart symbolism it is at the centre of the cross – point of unity. Completion, love, life, creation, beauty. Sacred to many deities, religions, cultures. Meditation will reveal its mystery.

Round table The circle depicts equality, totality, perfection like the heavens. The Grail is its mystic centre. The twelve knights denote the signs of the Zodiac.

Shell Birth, regeneration, love/marriage, fertility. Feminine, watery principle. Scallop shell denotes pilgrimage, journey across sea. **Ship** Adventure, setting out on the sea of life or crossing the waters of death. Protection – as a cradle.

Silver The Moon. The feminine force or aspect. Purity. The queen (king is gold).

Sphere Perfection, the Soul, container of all possibilities in the world. No time, no space: eternity.

Sphinx Composed of various human parts and four animal parts: head of man/woman, body of a bull, feet of a lion, wings of an eagle. These represent the four elements, air, earth, fire and water, the four astrological signs of Aquarius, Taurus, Leo and Scorpio, said to be the four corners of the earth or Lords of Creation. A mysterious guardian symbol which unites earthly meanings with heavenly/spiritual knowledge, which is to be revealed during the Age of Aquarius.

Square The earth, earthly existence (note the circle – heaven – as its opposite). It represents the fixed, limited form – static perfection, e.g. enclosures, gardens, courtyards, buildings, temples. In one way, the physical body housing the Soul. In sacred architecture, it shows form and knowledge transcending the material world. (A study of sacred geometry reveals this flow of knowledge, as does meditating within a 'temple' structure or the physical body as the temple.)

Star Hope, protection, light shining in the darkness. A divine presence/angelic messenger. The five-pointed star is man aspiring upward towards illumination, the six-pointed star is the combination of the upward-pointing triangle of fire and masculinity and the downward-pointing triangle of water-feminine, denoting Creation. There are many more graphic details with hidden meanings for stars with further numbers of points worth researching. They can act as powerful protection symbols.

Steps Rising towards communication – to enter sacred space as in ascending the 'temple' steps, steps up to an altar, steps up to a throne, taking steps to achieve a goal or spiritual purpose. The stairway to paradise. Stepped pyramids denote the seven levels or heavens up the sacred mountain. Every step is significant in meditation.

Sun Life (rising) and death (setting). The centre of being – the Life Force. Individuality. Supreme cosmic power. In most traditions, the Sun is seen as universal Father, the Moon as Mother. Can be Great Spirit or a feminine mother power. Note the mysterious differences between the outward, visible Sun and the invisible, inner suns when meditating. The entrance to knowledge.

Swan Bird of life, divine and pure. Denotes solitude and retreat, music and poetry; combines elements of air and water. When 'seen' with chain of gold or silver around its neck, symbolises the appearance of a divine being. Many other complex meanings.

Sword Protection, power and authority. Masculine principle, active process of the will. The main metaphysical meaning is discrimination, to bring about right spiritual decisions and protect all that is sacred. Associated with the underwater/supernatural powers in myths and legends, e.g. Lady of the Lake and Excalibur.

Temple Dwelling place on earth of the Divine. The physical body is a 'temple' of the Soul. Meeting place between the 'above' and the 'below'. Temples are structured with harmony that reflects order and stability, indicating cosmic and religious connections depending on the particular traditions of expression.

Throne Implies the relationship between God and man, sovereign and man. The throne can be described as a higher level of attainment – seat of authority, responsibility and wisdom.

Tower Aspiration, moving to higher levels of awareness. Power and protection, isolation, retreat. Without preparation for such retreat, it can mean a prison. Vigilance is required (watch tower). An ivory tower: inaccessible.

Tree Important and complex: symbolises the whole in existence, the world centre and linking 'other' worlds. An axis with roots in the ground, trunk reaching upward with growing branches towards the heavens. Deciduous trees: the world in constant renewal. Evergreens: immortality, everlasting. Different species sacred to different traditions.

Triangle Shows the threefold nature of the Universe such as father, mother, and child, or body, Soul and spirit. The equilateral triangle depicts completion. Love, truth and wisdom. In Egypt, the triad is Osiris as the beginning, Isis as the receptacle and Horus as the accomplishing (the offspring of the two). This describes a right-angled triangle with the base, feminine, the perpendicular as male and the hypotenuse as the continuity or offspring. Meditation on this figure will produce much information.

Unicorn The single horn of the unicorn symbolises union/undivided power. The horn can detect poison in water and purify it. A mythical animal symbolising all moral virtues with strength of mind, goodwill and gentleness.

Vine Seen as a sacred symbol of life and fertility because of its speedy growth from the main stem, giving shade, fruit and, ultimately, wine. The mystical emblem of many deities.

Wall Both protecting and (as in a walled city) limiting content. A line of meeting between the outer and inner worlds. A definition, a boundary. Entering into the unknown as you go through the door in the wall. A wall of flame in metaphysical terms signifies protection.

Water The first form of matter and the source of life. Liquid light. Fire with water unites to bring about heat and moisture necessary for life. Protective, will surround and enclose sacred spaces keeping them pure. Moving, running water signifies the waters of life. Can create and destroy. Fluidity of life, rigidity of death. A subject to be researched and contemplated.

Whale Regeneration through the power of the cosmic waters. The idea of being swallowed by the whale is symbolic of entering into darkness, the abyss and returning after three days to new life. A sonic symbol – whales harmonise the waters through sound.

Wheel The passage of the Sun, with the Sun in the centre. The cycle of life. The wheel of fate or time. The wheel of the Zodiac divided into twelve sections. There is the attainment of being in the 'centre' and unmoved.

Wind The element air in movement. The breath of the Universe. Holy breath/spirit. Holding, intangible and elusive. Messengers of the gods: the presence of supernatural forces through the spiralling whirlwind.

Wings Spirituality, intelligence, evolution, the movement of communication. The flight of time and thought. Messengers such as angels, the god Mercury with winged feet, symbolise travel through air from 'another place'. The power to transcend the mundane world.

Yin-Yang Yin is the feminine and Yang the masculine principle and together they symbolise the perfect balance – each contains the germ of the other, the two powers contained within the circle – totality. Perfection of balance and harmony.

Zodiac A wheel depicting the cycle of a year contained in twelve equal sections. The signs of each section are symbolic of their nature. By decoding the information of the signs and the elements associated with them, an understanding of all 'points of view' to the centre (the Sun) can be facilitated. Each section has a different task to accomplish in a lifetime in relation to the whole. Meditation on the Zodiac can be very rewarding.

Summary

In our ordinary, outer life, we see the structure of the world as a place of *forms* – people, buildings, objects – anything is form. It can all be identified, described and filed.

In the inner worlds of meditation, things are experienced as *formless*. There is an unrestricting, limitless quality to these experiences. The forms can be introduced at the beginning by visualising them, but they then become other-dimensional, holographic and unlimited. One begins to unravel the secrets or mysteries behind the form – the symbol, sign, sacred geometry or pattern. Other images may appear as a result of the original meditational focus, which will often give deep, personal meaning. It is because the 'self' or consciousness has moved into the zone of *timelessness*.

Visualisation is necessary in order to really understand geometric forms. You will find that you can then perceive their energy field generating out of the shape once you lift your awareness from the flat, two-dimensional form as shown on paper.

Reconstruction in computer graphics helps to establish the different sides or 3D points of view – the form, but it can never give you the *feeling* energy field or experience of the total image. For that, you need to enter the timelessness of meditation.

All patterns have movement and all movement generates pattern. This is what happens in sacred dancing, circle dancing and anything where rituals are performed. A pattern or thought-form is being generated in that place of performance. No wonder there are heavy atmospheres left by wars, crimes of violence and horror which have impinged upon a place or area where they have left their pattern of energy. In contrast, where high-quality performances, rituals, prayers and joyful ceremonies have taken place, there are patterns left of harmony, tranquillity and peace. This is what you are creating and building in your own meditation room/space just by your active presence!

Finally, the examples in the mini-reference list of symbols can all be used as meditation tools for focus and concentration when the chosen symbol will unfold its hidden information. Let your intuition guide you through the list when making your choices, only doing one at a time. Using the opening procedure in the usual way, go to your peaceful garden or 'temple' and work from there, bringing the chosen symbol into picture form upon your inner screen. Don't force or become intense, try to retain your relaxed state with mental alertness and hold the image so that it can communicate with you. Be patient with yourself and ask for guidance from your Higher Self. Repeat the process with the same symbol for several sessions and see how, little by little, an understanding is revealed. When you return, write down all that you have experienced. In this way, your personal adventure will accumulate depth and strength.

8

The power of thought for self-healing

Upon that which you place attention, so power is given to it, therefore place attention on the goodness which will, by its very light, heal all else

What do we really mean by 'goodness'? One explanation is 'something which has the right qualities'. It is having positive excellence beyond compare, encompassing virtue and loving kindness. This quality of goodness radiates a loving, benevolent light frequency. It has radiating intelligence.

We often say that somebody or something needs some TLC or tender, loving care. This is what is required for *you* – your daily gift to yourself, even if you cannot set aside regular, daily meditation time, you can harness the healing powers of love each day in only minutes.

In this chapter we explore the tools and how to place our attention in order to apply some general healing to ourselves, no matter whether we are always healthy or suffering from a serious bodily affliction, or perhaps in-between the two with recurring health problems. The secret is to keep our frequencies as high as possible under any circumstances and thus, a lot of low level infection will just bounce off us. The most important point to remember is that energy management is energy maintenance which is preventive medicine.

In Chapter 2, we built up the picture of our third-dimensional spacesuit demonstrating that we are much, much more than just a physical body. The subtle bodies and chakras, in supporting and nourishing the physical body, need to receive our healing attention, for when blockages occur on those subtle levels and are not cleared, then there is only one place for ills to manifest – and that's the physical body!

There is a two-way process going on where the physical body needs food, water and air to just survive, but if the nourishment is of good quality – or full of 'goodness' where the food, water and air are fresh and pure – then the physical body's high energy frequency can be upheld. The minute we become tired or undernourished in any way, we open ourselves to physical or psychic infections which are operating on a lower energy frequency. Clearing blockages from the subtle bodies need not manifest totally through the physical body if the physical is in good vibrational order and if there is an opportunity to have healing or healing therapy.

Looking at everything in terms of its energy field is a simple way of understanding your own energy system and how much you can push yourself or get away with before exhaustion finally tests your immune system to breaking point. Even an inherited, genetic tendency can be re-programmed given enough TLC. (I have, and am personally working on this angle of self-healing for myself.) I have observed many people reliving the physical and emotional states of great-grandfathers, great, great-grandmothers and other ancestors. Each person had a painful injury which they were healing and while doing this realised that they were also releasing and healing the trauma of an ancestor who, in their time, may not have taken responsibility for their beliefs and actions. Of course, you can't blame the ancestors and the past. You are here and now and the very reason that they existed, having inherited many, fine, strong qualities. You are also in charge of the ancestors' DNA while you're in this body on the Earth and, by careful maintenance, can heal and improve it.

Ancestral energy blocks are most apparent in the lower parts of the body where they keep us from stepping into our true power. Any spinal articulation that is not freely moving will slow or block the process of clearing the DNA from genetic inheritances. Indeed, any back problem is a message from your body trying to tell you that some vital changes in your life are required. Just locate which chakra position is involved. Back problems will continue to recur throughout life unless you take charge of your Life Force.

We need to remind ourselves that behind all this information is the fact that we are here on earth to learn how to balance physicality and spirituality. Our ability to heal the physical body is a vital component already operating, as demonstrated when we cut ourselves and the wound eventually closes over and heals. The etheric body – the energy body to the physical – is one of the unseen mechanisms or storage batteries which is affected by cuts and wounds to the physical, as explained in Chapter 2. This body assists us when we are asleep or in meditation by regenerating itself while the physical is still or at rest. We can programme it to build its strength and this will resonate through the physical body, for all new ideas first form in the etheric body and are then released into the lower bodies.

To restore and maintain these different fields is simple.

If you like, play a tape of some slow, gentle background music that enhances your environment, sit in your quiet space and go into the opening procedure of breathing, relaxing and protecting. (If you think you will have difficulty remembering the following sequence then as before, read it very, very slowly onto a tape.)

Exercise 8: Power of Violet Fire of Peace

Think about your aura surrounding you. The etheric, emotional and mental bodies are closest to your physical body with their energy interpenetrating it and vibrating around you. Give a special focus to the etheric body and its goodness – how it balances and automatically works with all of your bodies. Imagine the etheric body gradually becoming a lilac-coloured balloon enclosing and permeating the physical body, the emotional and mental bodies. Its goodness is strength and love displaying this beautiful lilac washing through all of your bodies. Let it penetrate deeper and deeper until you can feel the strength and the love.

Now the colour of the etheric body intensifies to violet, slipping over and through your other bodies, one by one. This beautiful healing light and healing love permeates every cell of your physical body and washes through your emotional and mental bodies. Imagine the violet building and spilling out of your crown chakra at the top of your head. See it washing right down your chakra system ... this fire of violet healing light penetrates your crown ... brow ... throat ... heart ... solar plexus ... stomach area ... the base chakra ... washing down to the legs and feet ... Breathe it up and around your aura back up to the crown and letting the deep violet light wash all of your bodies with the deep goodness of unconditional love and healing light. Keep breathing in the violet light, quietly and gently to every part of your lower bodies ...

Your body is like a huge container now filled with the waters and the love of the Universe ... relax ... feel the strength and feel the love. As the vitality of the etheric body touches the physical body, know and understand that you are healed. You are healed and recharged and all is well ...

When you are ready, return to full consciousness by saying 'I am now closing down and all my bodies and chakras are fully protected in this Violet Light of the Universe'. Take some deep breaths … stretch and open your eyes.

Any time you need replenishment – *imagine* this idea wherever you may be. You can do it sitting on the bus or train, in the car before you set off for home at the end of the day or in the lunch hour when at work, lying on the beach, in the bath or standing in the supermarket queue. (In this case, you may have to keep your eyes open and just hold the focus.) It doesn't matter. If you and I are in the same queue – I'll know what you're doing – neither of us will be wasting valuable time. Just be sure to close down properly with the end statement as a precaution before you get to the check-out! Primarily, use this sequence for your meditation which will allow better relaxation and a deeper experience.

As your etheric body works its magic and you become replenished with the help of your mental and emotional bodies which are also replenished, you will feel love – unconditional love for yourself and everything in the world around you.

Exercise 9: First Aid for Pain/Discomfort
If you have a headache, a muscle pain or ache in the bones, or perhaps some digestive disorder, then try the following:
1   Don't dwell upon the reason *why* you're experiencing discomfort. Close your eyes.
2   Put up your protection.
3   Imagine the lilac bubble of the etheric body penetrating through all of the lower bodies and gradually deepen it to violet. Breathe violet fire all around yourself. Build it up and see it moving.
4   Focus on the area under stress and surround it with your outbreath of violet by breathing in a clockwise direction using imagination, making seven circles around the area.
5   Now with the in-breath, encircle the area with seven anti-clockwise circles. Imagine this powerful light penetrating and lifting every bit of pain and negativity from the area as you breathe in. Each time you breathe out, breathe straight down into the ground below your feet.
6   See the pain releasing, flowing and moving downward. It will not release outward or upward.

7   Finally, fill the area with seven more violet light circles in a clockwise direction.

8   Relax and be still a few moments telling yourself three times, 'My body is in harmony'.

9   Close down.

Your expectations may be such that the pain should be instantly gone, but it may take a little longer for your system to recognise the signals that have been programmed into it, plus the fact that because we live in the dense, third-dimensional state of life, there is a delay mechanism for the impulse to arrive at its destination. Remember, it may have taken you all day to manifest your tense headache, so be kinder to yourself and let everything you have programmed in settle down for about ten minutes or so. That's one less painkiller for your digestion to process.

Letting go of an attachment, like pain, can be quite difficult for some. It has perhaps become part of their survival system, but any attachment is unnecessary intensity – it creates a bond in itself. We can become too attached to anything *except* the Life Force of the Universe which is attached *to us* because we are a part of it. That Life Force is love. If that Life Force is denied, then we can lose ourselves, our destiny and our mission – everything. We need to forgive ourselves and others and thus release attachment. Encourage your body. Talk to it, don't blame it or yourself, love it by not resisting the natural healing qualities already present, within and around it. Bring them forth and let nature conduct the healing. The natural decay of the body is due to resistance to Life Force. That resistance is usually based on fear. Fear comes from constant indoctrination which overburdens our natural survival response of 'fight or flight'. The negative side of flight is involved with guilt, fear, inadequacy, insecurity and blaming both the self and others. We can analyse our patterns of resistance and distortions one by one if we choose, but the simple, direct route is to connect in your heart with your Soul's original purpose and power.

Nature is Life Force which has intelligence. Every cell, organ, each part of the body has its own innate intelligence or angel, that can correct and heal the body if we allow it. Self healing – just *doing it* with no strings attached and trusting in the abilities of the natural healing elements – will give all the bodies a sense of well-being and an opportunity to let go graciously of all unnecessary emotional and mental garbage.

If you want experts in healing light management, call on the angelic realms during your meditation and ask for assistance with releasing attachments.

Exercise 10: Let Go and Heal

Once more, after you're settled, relaxed and protected in your space, raise your left hand, palm pointing outward (as if pushing), and your right hand resting on your thigh with the palm upward. You will be releasing all negativity through the right hand.

Breathe in through your left hand. Become more and more relaxed, lighter and lighter. Allow the energy to flow in as you allow the Breath of Light and Life to flow in through your left hand, feel it entering into your body like a soothing warmth. Let your body gently expand and relax with every in-breath and begin to breathe out through your right hand. Let all restriction and negativity be released by your right hand, slowly breathing in through your left hand. Now release through your right hand.

As you release through the right hand, the Angels of Transmutation take it, collect it and surround it with love and light. Keep breathing in the Life Force slowly through the left hand, filling the body with light and letting go of all stress, all attachments and all negative energies in your body … releasing through your right hand … more and more relaxed … becoming peacefully still within your heart and mind … your heart is peaceful and filling with more and more joy … your mind is quiet and more peaceful with every breath you take in and release … Allow that which you are … to grow and become … as the breath in brings you strength … and the breath out releases all attachments and negativity…

Now, as you breathe in the gift of life through your left hand, allow yourself to send your deepest desires out through your right hand. Feel the rhythm of life in your breath – breathing in life and love, breathing out your needs, breathing in life, love and peace … breathing out your needs with peace and love … breathing in life, love and peace … breathing out your needs with peace and love …

Stay in this regular, slow, breathing pattern and if you would like a corrective, healing re-alignment from the angelic frequencies breathe in the Life Force and breathe out the request through your right hand. Relax your left hand and rest it on your left thigh, palm upwards. Relax and focus the breath in the heart area with your

Higher Self and the angelic realms who will hold you safely … as you let go… (At this point the reactions may be gentle tears of joy or you may feel a finger or thumb give a little twitch or a subtle spasm/shudder in your body – it will be hardly noticeable if it happens at all, but just know that you are warm and safe.)

When you are ready, you will return to full consciousness feeling peaceful and calm. You are now closing down. Count down from twelve to one, visualising the appropriate chakras, remembering to place on each one the gold disc with the cross etched upon it, then down to your knees, feet and Earth Star. Place a warm cloak around yourself, pulling the hood over your head. Take some deep breaths, stretch and open your eyes.

As before, this exercise should be done in your chair in the meditation seated position, so that your feet are rooting you in to the ground. You may want to hold the left arm close to your body to get some support for it as it is held in the upright position.

The healing power of nature

The tree/plant kingdom and the mineral kingdom of this planet both assist and nurture the animal and human kingdoms with their particular unseen energies. We know we should not survive without the presence of trees to absorb carbon dioxide and emit oxygen, but there are other, deeper aspects to trees, plants and flowers.

The ancients understood the spirit of trees and developed working relationships with them simply because they revered all life. They knew that trees had existed before man and that they held great accumulated wisdom of tree lore. The auras of trees can be felt with practice and it is a very good exercise to go out into a park or the countryside to become more aware of the living spirit in all trees and plants. Man is always taking from nature without giving much back, so a right attitude of exchange is essential for the serious seeker. To feel the power of a tree, choose those with a very active aura like an oak, ash or silver birch tree. Stand a few metres away from your chosen specimen and observe and admire the way it looks, its shape and majesty. Mentally tune in to it, asking the tree if you can experience its energy. (Just because it's rooted to the spot doesn't in any way diminish its intelligent energy.) Move forward slowly and keep pausing to feel the different bands of energy emanating from its aura. They form outward-moving circles. Only continue if the feeling is positive. When you feel a positive response, move closer towards the trunk and sit down with your back against it. (If you feel uncomfortable about your first choice/ there is no response, then seek another suitable tree.)

As you sit with your back to the tree – or if you prefer, you can stand – fully relax your body against the tree trunk, breathing more and more rhythmically as you sense the Life Force within the trunk rising upward towards the branches. Ask the tree for its support and feel gratitude for the work that it does as you become at one with the tree. Relax more and more as the strength of the tree's Life Force enfolds you and you can feel its power running down your spine. You should feel an inner warmth and peace. Take at least twenty minutes to half an hour breathing and meditating with the tree, after which you should convey your gratitude to it. You should feel invigorated.

This action of joining forces with nature in meditation produces a silent power within you, akin to that which your ancestors knew. A healing takes place. (Ignore any negative remarks from those who are not so well-informed for they deny the Life Force freely available to all.)

You can replicate this scenario in a meditation by entering your garden sanctuary through your door and finding the tree and then becoming one with it in the same way. In this case you will be receiving the energy through the ether on a different level. As a physical person concerned with your well-being on a third-dimensional level of existence, it might be a wise experiment to do it both ways and compare your notes. The healing essence of the ash tree will awaken your intuition and convey a more refined awareness while the birch will strengthen you in times of difficulty with the essence of determination. All trees have particular strengths in the same way plants have healing powers and once more, you only need to tune in with respect and ask!

The Tree of Life is a symbol coming from ancient religious traditions to the present day. All religions have aspects which are seen in their buildings, rituals and writings, and there are also those aspects which are hidden from general view. These form the sacred, original seeds or principles from which different expressions of fervour develop in the hands and minds of successive generations. The inner tradition of the Tree of Life is said to have come directly from the Source who instructed angels to form the pattern and principles for instruction to mankind. Studying these principles reveals a spiritual pathway of immense depth.

The Tree of Life or Cosmic Tree appears as a prime symbol in many different religions with varying archetypal and sacred meanings attached to different species.

Crystals: the mineral kingdom

This powerful section of the world of nature is well worth looking at if you haven't already discovered its gifts.

Meditating with crystals brings support to your personal energy field and they will boost, heal and regenerate all of your bodies.

The family of quartz crystal are the most common and best for all-round use. For meditation or power breathing, hold a piece of quartz in your left hand to uplift your energy field after a strenuous day and find a good-size cluster of amethyst to keep in your sacred meditating space to radiate the healing violet colour. Amethyst is renowned for collecting negativity in an environment. All crystals need regular washing and cleansing if you use them for healing and meditating and different crystals each give a particular healing quality. Blue lace agate and snowy (milky) quartz both emit peace and tranquility as part of their energy field, while rose quartz gives a peaceful, loving vibration. Further study of the power of crystals is highly recommended. The world of nature holds all that we need to sustain and develop mind, body and spirit, no matter what our point of view.

Reprogramming for health, using affirmations

If we were perfect, we wouldn't be here on the Earth, for we are here to learn and experience life through the most powerful essence within us – which is the Life Force. This connects us to everything and as we move through life we bring this essence of ourselves to everything and everyone we touch, expressing it through the physical body with our emotions and through the mind with our thoughts. This means that the physical body, as the temple of our being, needs to be cared for properly so that the thoughts we think are filled with as much Life Force as possible – and vice versa; our thinking needs to be only positive and commanding to send the right messages to the body through the brain.

Affirmations are positively marvellous for bringing about right attitude, intention and focus. We are setting up new files in our brain computer which are instructing us accordingly. These will not only programme the subconscious mind but they are also energy thought-forms being sent out into the Universe.

If affirmations are stated over and over again, they become a part of you. (Did anyone keep telling you that you were stupid when you were a child – or something similar?) To counteract and cleanse negative programming from your individual system you really have to go for it in a big way since you are transforming old patterns and building a new inner structure all at the same time. Make a rule to repeat your affirmation(s) on waking, before you start the day or in your morning meditation. You can start by affirming who and what you are. Here are some examples :

* I am – and what I am is evolving in harmony with the Life Force.
* I am a spiritual being experiencing the Life Force in a physical body.
* My mind, body and spirit have beauty, goodness and truth.
* I believe in my 'self' and my inner reality and bring this into outer manifestation.

It is necessary to be clear about what you wish to empower and become responsible for your actions and reactions, so bring some strength of feeling to this affirmation:

* I am in charge of my actions and reactions to people and events in my life.

If you are blown away by other people and their 'attitude' then this might be a useful one. If someone makes you very angry – who is in charge here? To recognise emotional action in others and not to join in is the mark of being in charge of yourself. You can always agree to disagree with another and then walk away. You will have retained your energy for more worthy causes – yours. To acknowledge the Life Force and to keep it free-flowing throughout your body is a vital health message:

* I am the Life Force within, connecting to the Life Force of the Universe. I radiate health to every cell of my body.

Affirmations aren't *begging* in their message either. They are statements of truth – your truths which may have been forgotten long, long ago and are re-surfacing, or they are statements of intent 'as if' something is already certain.

Having a goal, an aim in life, means you have already dreamed about the idea of what you want. Be consistent and keep affirming. This will really prove whether you have a commitment to yourself or if you are still hoping that the Universe will provide willy-nilly without any effort at all. The Universe is merely waiting for your positive request and your ability to magnetise your requirements to you – that is your effort.

Remember 'like attracts like'? Be careful and as wise as you can with your dreams. A dream that is a positive, creative energy will succeed in time, but you have to keep energising it. The lower ego will try to set up some opposition to these new ideas and tell you that the whole idea is silly, what will people think, you're going mad and so on. Be prepared and strengthen your resolve to go beyond the lower ego and bring all of your greater 'I am' presence into your life:

✱ I am dedicated to promoting the Life Force throughout my being. In so doing, I know it will be radiated to others.

✱ Today, I feed the Life Force to my mind, body and spirit. I am radiating health. And so it is.

Affirmations need to be repeated for many weeks with resolve – visualise or imagine it happening. One affirmation should be repeated *three* times. Make up your own carefully in accordance with your needs and circumstances – and do it!

Summary: the main points to observe in self healing

1. **Attitude** Creating a relaxed, positive attitude so that your Life Force can flow freely to prevent decay setting in. Old, outworn ideas, fear programming etc., have got to go.

2. **Intention** The decision to take charge of your own life and to become quite clear as to who is responsible for your own physical body. Re-programme towards your greater picture.

3. **Focus** Mind your own business. What is right for one person in any moment is not necessarily right for another. Although it may seem obvious to you – you could be wrong. Everyone has their own timing and their own type of courage. Really knowing your own response timings to outside influences is in this learning curve. Keep your ailments in positive alignment to your intent to heal yourself. This means not dissipating your energies in discussions about the worst possible scenarios in your future or the future of others.

The future is yet to be written and you bring both the past and the present with you to create the script. If you feel frail and needful, that's OK too – just keep in constant dialogue with your Higher Self, asking for help to place in your path the person or event that can help your circumstances and encourage you for your *highest possible good*. Trust in the Life Force at your command.

Part Three
FINE TUNING

9

The power and importance of colour and sound

Everything is in a process of change evolving from one thing to another. Finding ways of maintaining balance in this flow is the art of living with wisdom

Colour and sound are complementary to each other, for they are pulses of energy carrying the same kind of electrical potential. This expresses itself to us through the application of our brain recognising these rhythms through our physical senses of seeing and hearing. We know the ranges of both colour and sound extend way beyond our ordinary senses. When an altered state of consciousness is achieved through meditation, then these higher and finer frequencies can be experienced to some extent on the higher levels of the whole of our being, where they can be very quickly assimilated for healing and toning up the body.

The human race has already developed great awareness and skill regarding the world of colour from scientific through to practical, daily uses. The development of sound in using sonic devices (scientific, medical, healing), through to the various expressions of music, are ever-changing and developing.

Music (sound) and art (colour) can touch the Soul – our innermost core.

Through pursuing our own personal development of our extrasensory skills, we can reawaken latent talents involving the finer frequencies of colour and sound through mind training and focus, using the practice of creative meditation.

We are only using 18–20 per cent of our brains right now. The rest is really asleep. We know that we have physical limitations and this is one of the reasons. By claiming back that which has been lost, we gradually re-awaken our extra-sensory skills. For example, in meditation we may experience 'seeing' or being part of colourful scenarios or we may 'see the light', be surrounded by it, or step into it – an all-pervading peaceful and loving experience. This can occur because we have let go of our third-dimensional physical restraints by relaxation, focus and intent, thus expanding our abilities into a wider range of 'seeing' and experiencing beyond the density of third-dimensional matter. The problem is – and it's only a small one – that colours are often experienced in meditation that have no name and therefore, no identification because they are 'out of this world' and its colour language. We are only familiar with third-dimensional languages for descriptive purposes.

So, we humans only experience colour basics, yet we are operating in a 3D spacesuit which holds unlimited potential where it is possible to harness a wider range of sound and colour. These possibilities are all very well, but first, do we know enough and can we feel the potential hidden in the basics, let alone the greater picture? Perhaps it is better to strengthen the rainbow bridge with practice and eventually cross easily into these uncharted lands rather than blow the mind with psychadelic buzz. The Power of Peace, when you find it, is a far greater prize.

Colour co-ordinating

We have already introduced the healing power of violet light into our meditations for self-healing, but now we extend our inner colour visualisations for some finer tuning. To make this further connection to colour, let us remind ourselves first of the colours of the seven-chakras system of our bodies, the colours of the rainbow: 1. Red (base); 2. Orange (sacral); 3. Yellow (solar plexus); 4. Green (heart); 5. Blue (throat); 6. Indigo (brow); 7. Violet (crown).

Now look at the way the colours mix themselves and therefore interact. The base colour is red, the colour of life – the life blood. Move up the column and see how red and yellow make orange, yellow and blue make green, and blue and violet make indigo. Beyond the head the spectrum merges to become light. Quite simply, there is an ongoing development showing in chakra colours as they mix and match. With our day-to-day 'working' of the physical body resulting in many experiences, so the colours refine and mature and when we decide to bring light into each chakra, re-align ourselves and start to take care of our subtle bodies, so the physical is aligned with the spiritual parts of us, which brings maturity, wisdom and knowledge into our whole being. We are claiming back that which has been lost.

To recap: in our opening procedure for meditation, we connect with the Soul Star above the head and breathe down light energy through the chakras to connect with the Earth Star below the feet. Thus we create a tube or a beam of light which runs through each chakra in the centre of our body, down to below our feet to be grounded.

To enhance the quality of each chakra and eventually develop this beam into a Pillar of Light, the chakras need to be cleansed regularly and therefore, your colour system will gradually clarify and your Life Force circulate more freely. In order to become more familiar with the colour sequence of the chakras, try the following meditational exercise.

Prepare yourself as usual, with relaxation, breathing and protection after settling into your space.

Exercise 11: Chakra Colour Feeling
Outside noises will not disturb you.

In front of you is your door ... Grasp the handle of the door and open it. Move over the threshold and close the door behind you. In front of you is a pathway of light which leads to a red door. Move along the pathway and touch the red door with your hand. It opens ... Enter over the threshold.

You are standing in a large room where everything is coloured in shades of red from scarlet through to deep rose-red – the carpet, curtains and so on. It is cosy and warm. Pause ... breathe in red and remember how red feels to you (pause) ... Do not linger, but move towards the door opposite coloured orange. Touch it to open and move into this room. All around you everything is in shades of orange, from pale peach to deep apricot and the vibrant colour of oranges. Pause ... breathe in orange and remember how orange feels to you (pause) ... Do not linger but move to the door opposite, coloured yellow. Touch it to open and move into this room. It is like walking into sunlight with all the yellow tinges from deep cream through to deep daffodil yellow and shafts of golden light come through the windows. Pause ... breathe in yellow/gold and remember how it feels to you (pause) ...

Do not linger but move to the door opposite, coloured green. Touch it to open and move into this room. Feel the softness and peace of very pale green through to all the deeper shades of nature. A pale pink shaft of light pours through the window. All is peace.

Pause ... breathe in the green and remember how it feels (pause) ... Once more ... do not linger but move to the door opposite, coloured blue. Touch it to open, and pass into this room. You are surrounded by all the shades of blue from pale to turqoise and through to clear sky blue. Feel the clarity. Pause and breathe in the blue and remember how it feels (pause) ... Do not linger but move towards the door opposite coloured indigo – a deep, dark blue with a purple tinge. Touch the door to open it and move into this room. Feel the warmth and space of indigo wrap gently around you. Breathe in ... remember how indigo feels to you (pause) ...

Do not linger but move to the final door opposite, coloured violet. Touch it to open and pass into this room. Let all the shades, from pale lilac through to violet, pervade your being. Let the peace and tranquillity enter through your breath. Breathe in the silence and stay in that silence, knowing you are becoming more and more balanced. Remember the colour of violet ... (pause for a minute) ...

Now gently re-focus on the door opposite – a golden door. Touch it to open and pass through. The door closes behind you. There are steps descending into your own peaceful garden. Move down them and along the pathway to your own personal door. Stand there and look down at yourself. You are wearing a 'cloak of many colours'. You have brought all the colours back with you!

Hanging beside the door, there is the usual darker cloak. Place it around you, pulling the hood over your head. It feels warm and protective. Open your door and pass through, closing it behind you. You will remember all the colours and how you felt in their presence.

You are now returning to full consciousness with the countdown from twelve and placing the golden disc with the cross as a seal upon each chakra as each number is said (slowly): 12 ... 11 ... 10 ... 9 ... 8 ... 7 ... 6 ... 5 ... 4 ... 3 ... 2 ... 1 ... down to the knees, each foot and to the Earth Star ... Take some deep breaths, move hands and feet ... stretch ... and open your eyes. Without speaking, write down your impressions of the colours and if you found any of them easy or difficult.

Having read through this exercise, read it slowly as usual onto a tape for your own use. This exercise will establish your inner colour presence and also connect with the health needs of your physical body. Each chakra, as we observed in Chapter 2, is connected to a particular gland of the body and by doing this colour visualisation we are making a deeper, conscious connection with our Life Force.

Even just reading it through slowly will have a positive impact, although it is much more rewarding and exciting to go for the experience.

As the crown chakra 'room' of violet is reached, there is an opportunity to merge with the silence and focus solely upon that space. It is here where the mystery of the Power of Peace is illumined, a unique experience for each person and not something which can be described with words. Every exercise and meditation in this book is leading you ultimately to this space.

Of course, because this whole exercise forms a basic idea for chakra cleansing, it might be a good idea at this stage to remind yourself about the chakra details by going back to Chapter 2 and re-reading their functions.

Once you feel comfortable about moving through the chakra 'rooms', try the following variations to bring in the refining qualities of light as you learn more about yourself.

Exercise 12: The Light Bearer
Enter the meditation through your door as usual and, on the other side of the door, collect a basket filled with seven spheres of healing light. The basket is waiting on the pathway leading to the red door. Pick it up and proceed as before, touching the door to enter the 'red room'.

Take one of the spheres of light from the basket and place it in the centre of the room, where it radiates white, silver and gold rays. Mentally request that the rays penetrate to every part of the room to cleanse and re-vitalise it. Continue your journey through every room, leaving a sphere at each centre with the same request. Leave through the final, gold door, move down the steps into your garden, placing the basket beside the pathway. Complete all your closing down procedures.

Exercise 13: Chakra Spring Cleaning
You may like to choose one particular chakra for personal development or healing, so enter the meditation as before through your own door, but then see the colour door of your choice ahead and enter by touch.

Stay and explore the contents of the room, changing and creating in a positive way, finding out just what 'stuff' has been hidden or accumulated and needs to be cleared.

The tools for transforming the room to clarity and the varieties of its colour is in your breath and intent. Breathe in light and breathe it out into the room or into a dark corner as required. Remember, you can create and re-create with the colour range of this chosen chakra or introduce other colours into the room if that is what is required for a healing. Ask for your Higher Self to assist you or ask the angel (the energy) of the chakra to work with you.

When you are in the chosen room in the meditation, you may like to sit down in the centre, choosing an appropriate chair, and breathe slowly and rhythmically to enter into further contemplation of the meaning of this chakra and its needs. You may become aware of the physical organs involved with this chakra, and information about stress, pain in the area and so on, will become apparent.

When you are ready to leave, the gold door appears opposite you, touch it and re-enter your garden. Closing down procedures as before.

Colour in clothes, furnishings and room decor can play an enhancing or manipulating role in our lives, depending on whether we are 'in tune' with a colour. Our feelings of well-being and comfort, or in contrast, irritation, exhaustion and 'ill-being' are constantly due to the effects of colour upon our individual energy field.

Everyone has their colour likes and dislikes which are really born out of their basic colour coding, for everyone has their own individual colour combination. This may consist of two or more colours which are the colour signature of that person and to which they will respond throughout life. These combinations describe the expressive quality of the personality and spirituality of a person, which is not quite the same as the aura where the swirling emanations of changing colours around the body describe the present feelings, state of health and spiritual health.

Of course, many people share the same code combination which doesn't necessarily bring them permanently closer or together; it merely states that their expressive roles in life will be similar and they will feel comfortable when in the company of each other. It is more than likely that their Soul missions coincide and they were destined to meet in this lifetime.

In Chapter 4 basic colours were recommended to use for certain kinds of protection. The importance of colour lies in the type of radiation each colour emits. When used in the imagination for meditational purposes, the power has a finer frequency. Colours used for decoration or for wearing in the physical world are more dense and flat. Once you have an idea of what colours are doing, and can do, with the type of power they are radiating, you can relate better to them on both the inner and the outer worlds and use and identify with them accordingly.

The following list of colours is a guideline to show some of their symbolic meanings and other effects particularly when experienced in meditation:

Red Passion, love, faith, health, strength. Sexual creativity, fertility. Fire Element, warming. Masculine, active principle. Enlivening, arousing. Raises blood pressure. Planet/God Mars. Anger, vengeance.

Orange Lifts and balances, enhances feelings. Invigorates and compels attention. Flame of love brings happiness. Stimulating, joyful. Promotes digestion. Rejuvenating.

Yellow Light of the Sun. Radiating in action, energising with inner warmth. Intellect, intuition, optimism, faith, goodness. Air element. Stimulates the nervous system.

Green Harmony. It brings blue and yellow into balance. Abundance, fertility, spring, nature, paradise, peace. The fairy colour. Spiritual growth. Can show as change or decay in poor, dark colour and renewal of life in fresh, bright colour.

Pink Peace and harmony. Pure love, compassion.

Blue Truth, wisdom, peace, loyalty. Infinite space, eternity. Sky gods. Queens of Heaven. Feminine principle. Water Element. Colour of Venus. Promotes healing, reduces blood pressure. The light of peace.

Violet Knowledge, intelligence, spiritual devotion, humility and balance. Sincerity, dignity. Relaxing blue with stimulating red gives balance to consciousness.

Purple Sovereign power, royalty. Justice, truth. Religious and ceremonial (rituals).

Brown Earth Element, ground force. Renunciation, penitence. Enclosing, integration. Practical.

Silver The Moon. Feminine principle. Reflective, mysterious. With gold shows two aspects of the same reality.

Gold The Sun. Masculine principle. Radiating. Divine power, immortality. Glorious.

White Purity. Protection – it insulates against intrusive energies.

Now think of the idea that very dense, dark colours have molecules which are closely packed together and have no space between them. As the colour lightens and changes, so the structure becomes looser and there is more space through which the finer, etheric energies can flow. This is a very simple way of understanding the process of healing and lightening up your body.

The magic of sound

Every cell in the human body has the capacity to respond to sound *outside* itself and also with the sound of the voice *within* that human body. The response by the cells is that they resonate with those sounds as they happen.

We identify with it in a positive or negative way, according to our own personal colour/sound patterns and our belief systems.

Sound is a most powerful tool to boost an idea and therefore a thought-form. We experience this when a particularly attractive piece of music is used as a background to a television commercial. It makes the idea of the commodity being advertised more memorable or pleasant. The sound drives the message home. It can have a deep effect on our whole body. The advertiser knows that you will retain the music or the song and thus identify with the commodity more powerfully.

In the same way, the chanting of sacred music, the repetition of sacred words or divine names on a note, or the toning of sounds creates a patterned thought-form to invoke the power which is sought, to enhance and experience the higher, spiritual nature. It is food for the Soul. It gets us in the right mood and mode for giving and receiving sound.

The word *mantra* describes the chanting of a divine name or names being repeated over and over again, sometimes accompanied by appropriate music. We can appreciate all the pleasant sounds but what about the unpleasant ones? There are ranges of sounds which are very detrimental to the human body and which promote stress. Some are audible, some inaudible to our hearing range. By using our voices more, we can bring sound from within ourselves to resonate our own cells when outside sounds are throwing us off-balance and into distress and irritation. Try it in the car!

Humming is good for you.

Each chakra in the seven colour chakra system resonates to a note on the scale: red = the note C, orange = D, yellow = E, green = F, blue = G, indigo = A, violet = B.

This is a basic format to use as an experimental starting point.

Just by sounding or humming the notes as you visualise the colour of the chakra, is enough to clear and re-align them. The sounds resonate on all the levels of invisible, etheric chakras. Any physical needs in the area of the chakra will receive healing. An over-all effect of well-being and peace pervades, and you can do this for yourself for free! Sound is safe to use for it works through the natural resonance of your body. Your own sound cannot damage your chakras or force them open. (If the intent is right, you automatically won't make sounds which you dislike or that make you feel uncomfortable.)

There are many different systems which work equally well and which you may like to research, but there is no need to feel inhibited by the thought that you have to learn to stick to one course. We really need to experiment to find the sequence of sound which works best for us because of our uniqueness.

The next development with sounding is to use the vowel sounds of A, E, I, O, U, plus two more sounds of AAH and UH to complete the seven. This is the order of these sounds and the relevant chakras:

1   Base chakra: UH (as in Huh).
2   Sacral chakra: OO (U).
3   Solar plexus chakra: OH (O).
4   Heart chakra: AH (as in ARE).
5   Throat chakra: EYE (I).
6   Brow chakra: AYE (A).
7   Crown chakra: EE (E)

These sounds link to harmonics – notes sounding compatable together – thus widening the effect.

You don't *have* to keep to the scale for vowel sounding but start with the deepest note you can make for the base chakra and then move up. By experimenting, you can hear and feel the body responding. When you mentally direct your sound to the particular chakra you have in mind, then things really get going. Listening to a high-quality record or tape of people sounding and toning, while you are in your meditation space in a relaxed mode, can shift your consciousness quite quickly, because the gradual build-up of energy in the room and in your body is brought about by the type of sound and the harmonics employed.

It is wise to think about what you intend before you start, as you are within a set of conditions which can be used for many benefits;

for example, you can use it as a kind of 'sound bath' for your own healing, or for a friend or family member who needs support. With right intent, sound can be of great benefit to everyone and everything. Be inventive – let your sound take the Power of Peace around the world, for sound is a tool for creation. The OM or AUM is said to be the most powerful sound and is sacred and universal, bringing and holding a state of peace and balance.

Many people sound this three times before meditating as it clears and prepares both the person and the space around them. If possible, try this and see what difference occurs in your body and your meditating space.

Generally, people feel inhibited for one reason or another finding it difficult to sing or sound, but start off with humming and you'll soon progress towards opening your mouth. The benefits of being able to clear your aura, the room, and restoring your own Life Force are only a few of the advantages waiting for you to discover them.

Music, rhythm, melody and harmony

Music should have rhythm, melody and harmony when used to clear unwanted negativity in a room or house, prior to meditation and should be in the middle to higher range of notes. If music is used during meditation, it should always be of a suitable type which provides a soft, inspirational background, raising the vibrations of the area in which you work. (Incessant, loud, discordant music is very detrimental to health and can damage chakras and other sensitive areas of the body. The Life Force is leached.)

Rhythm is the pulse of life – the heartbeat. Drums, rattles, bells and other percussion instruments activate different parts of the body; the rattle used by North American Indians, for example, is a cleansing instrument which loosens negative energy patterns when shaken around the body (the aura). Other healing methods are then applied.

Melody is a collection of tones which soothe and can alter emotional and mental stress. Humming and singing to yourself restores balance in or after experiencing stressful conditions.

Harmony encompasses the physical, emotional mental and spiritual aspects of sound. It is the key to altering, transmuting, raising or lowering and shifting our energies on all levels by affecting subtle and spiritual frequencies which align them with the physical aspects of our energy field.

Finding the right chord (two or more notes) which blend, can stabilise all systems of the body, bringing them into resonance with one another. When two or three people create and harmonise their voices and sound/sing a simple chord, they can clear low-level atmospheres in buildings or in places in the environment.

One person can achieve a good change but the correct pitch is needed and this should be studied and practised for proper benefit.

The value of combining colour and sound in meditation work is increasing as more and more people learn to let the voice come through as an expression of their energy.

It is a very ancient art and will be the most powerful of skills to be perfected and utilised in the coming years.

The Sri Yantra shape created
by sounding 'OM' – 'mmmm–o–mmmm'.
The triangles are created by 'mmmm',
the circle by 'o' (as in 'oh!').

10

The rhythm of life: tuning in for harmony

Rather ask – what does life mean to me, than to ask 'what is the meaning of life'

While our physical bodies pulse with the rhythm of life through our heartbeat, we have a lot of living to do – that is the job – to experience the laws of creation in the form we inhabit. Our third-dimensional spacesuit holds all the reference files we can ever need to access, in order to function with awareness. We have already seen how the chakras illustrate all the possibilities of growth and development in supporting the physical body and the subtle bodies. By calling in the finer, divine frequencies through our Higher Self in meditation, a safe journey is ensured.

We are rainbow (chakras) warriors, seeking the pot of gold (the crown) to go through the spectrum of visibility and beyond, into the loving peace of white light. (Aren't we really learning, little by little, how to 'beam ourselves up'?)

The search for meaning to our existence through meditation is undoubtedly the most important and simplest act we can do for self-discovery. It imparts a sense of order, alleviates boredom or frustration and provides a haven where we can heal and regenerate ourselves. By giving ourselves this opportunity, we access a silent power. It is the ability to tune ourselves in to the harmonic frequencies which feed our personal growth and Life Force.

To take this a step further, rather than look at what the meaning of life is in an abstract way, we can become at one with our Life Force through the Power of Peace and respond positively to all the unfolding opportunities, dramas and adventures which we attract to ourselves.

In other words, if we can find ways of tuning in and bringing harmony into the frame, then the Soul lessons we will undoubtedly encounter on the way will show meaning and purpose to our life jouney.

Through meditating with our Higher Self, they can be recognised, understood and become more acceptable as events and circumstances we have agreed to explore and harmonise in this lifetime. This contract is one of destiny. It is not something which is fated or written in stone to be accomplished one way and in one time frame. We have eternity to accomplish the greater mission, but one lifetime in which to wake up and work this part of the mission positively and creatively. No matter how old a person is in physical or spiritual years, this refining process is ever present, for it is the process of evolution and creation.

To change and take a different pace, or to take time to explore a different point of view is not to opt out of life but to be able to have the courage to stand back and choose an alternative route for your destiny.

Life without challenge and tension would be meaningless in the same way that life with an over-abundance of it becomes so. Finding the right key to attain balance is the challenge and then tension vibrates with harmony, like a chord correctly tuned and then played.

The pulse of life

The physicist W. Schumann discovered back in 1952 that the the planet Earth had a natural pulse beating at 7.83Hz which resonated around the planet. In the early space programmes it was found that astronauts had health problems on their return to Earth, so NASA installed magnetic pulse generators into all manned spacecraft to simulate and maintain a natural and healthy environment which balanced the Life Force of the astronauts (Schumann Simulators). Being out of tune with the earth's signal was obviously found to create imbalance and disharmony.

Back on Earth, the human body naturally synchronises with this magnetic pulse but is inhibited by the large amounts of electromagnetic pollution (radiation) in the environment. This has been found to interfere and lower the Life Force which can create health problems. (Has the earth's pulse now changed? Find out and get up-to-date.) In the simple act of meditation we can more consciously renew our natural, heartbeat connection with the Earth's pulse – her heartbeat, but this is only part of our Life Force story.

The *full* background Life Force of Earth, Sun, Moon and planets – our solar system, can be described as a giant, complex generator which is always helping us to maintain our life support systems. We shall be meditating upon our solar system and space, later in the chapter, to find out what this means to us personally.

Physically tuning in

In taking ourselves into the peace of the countryside and walking on the Earth we are unconsciously making a connection with the Earth pulse.

Have you noticed how gardening has become more and more popular? This is another way people are making their connection to Earth and working with the seasons. In swimming, especially in the natural waters and the oceans, standing under or near waterfalls and in climbing hills and mountains – we make our connections with our home – the planet Earth.

The ancient peoples of the world, our ancestors, all knew how to work and live this pulse and rhythm consciously and they honoured the order and the cycles of time, using them as a calendar and code. Their survival depended upon it.

In our genes we carry their knowledge which is forever in the background of our man-made, fast, technological world. Science and mythology, astrology and astronomy are closely interconnected in human history.

A typical biorhythms chart

Biorhythms

The discovery of three distinct biorhythmic cycles in man relate in the following way:

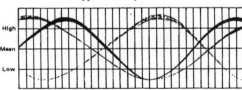

a   a physical energy cycle lasting twenty-three days.
b   an emotional, 'feeling' cycle lasting twenty-eight days.
c   a mental, intellectual cycle of thirty-three days.

These biorhythms can be found by looking at the positions of the Sun, Moon and the planet Mercury at a person's time of birth:

a   Sun = physical Life Force.
b   Moon = emotional, feeling personality
c   Mercury = the way of thinking and communicating.

The cycles are of the same length for everyone and they continue in the same manner throughout life. These rhythms will overlap at

123

different times for each individual according to the position of these three planetary bodies on the personal biorhythmic chart. Placed upon a graph, one can see the heights and troughs of each of the three energies and where they intersect with each other. Where these intersections occur there is least balance. The lower periods are recuperative leading to the higher, 'peak' performance days.

Biorhythms show the distinct path of our metabolic rate, based on only three planetary bodies while astrology takes all of the planets into account as well as fixed stars. The value of biorhythms lies in their simplicity of use.

Natal astrology

Astrology is an objective technique of interpretation which takes the meaning of the planetary cycles and relates them to possibilities for development and growth for the individual.

An astrological chart shows a more complex map of a person's field of operation which is described by setting out a chart of the planetary bodies at the very moment of birth. As a baby takes its first breath on Earth, the pattern is 'frozen'. This resulting pattern forms the basic map for interpretation, using the symbolism of planets and signs.

An astrologer works with this very complex system by using mathematical calculations, and devoting years of study to the meanings and symbolism of the signs and planets. The art is thousands of years old, when astrology and astronomy were not separated as they are today.

*Example of an astrological chart
(before birth)*

The influences of the planetary positions at the time of birth upon the individual chart will reveal not only characteristics, strengths and weaknesses, but indications as to the life mission. It is a unique map.

Upon that map can be applied the daily movements of the Sun, Moon and planets as they make angles to the chart. These will show periods of troughs, lows and equilibrium which can be calculated for the past, present and future, because the cycles and positions of each body in the sky is already known. (They are set out in an Ephemeris which anyone can purchase.) Hence one can look for the most opportune times ahead to make progress in life.

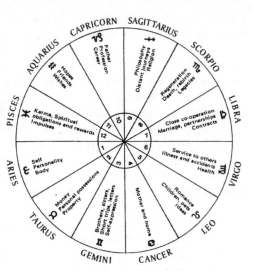

In both cases, using biorhythms and astrology, there is a clear case for gaining insight into one's personal cycles and rhythm of life. It is up to the individual how to use this information creatively and work with the symbolism in meditation.

The twelve houses in a chart showing how they resonate to the archetypes behind each astrological sign

You can see that newspaper and magazine horoscopes, which only use Sun signs, can barely touch on the matter. Fun turns into fact, when the complexities and information that an individual chart will reveal with the positions of all of the planetary bodies, form the whole, ongoing picture.

Astronomy provides the basic framework giving points of reference to calculate the planets and other celestial bodies in relation to Earth – the geocentric measurements where all is 'seen' from the viewpoint of Earth. Wonderful cosmic observations have been achieved through advances in technology which, together with space programmes, continue to inform us about the development of our Universe on the physical level of understanding. The work accomplished by astrophysicists deals with worlds not seen by the naked eye such as magnetic fields, ionised particle streams and vibrationary frequencies. Very often it is this world that the meditator taps into.

Although there are many ways of observing and researching into matters of space, we are all caught up in the business of the rhythm of life, being here and now with as many points of view and skills as

125

there are people in the world. Everything has its place in the unfolding of the human psyche.

The Sun

The Sun, at the edge of the Milky Way, as the life-giving force, is vital to life on Earth, as we are well aware.

On Earth, as we live out our days within the sun's field of influence, the observations of sunspots, solar winds and other surface activities are being calculated and measured for their subsequent effects to Earth and its life forms. The yearly Sun cycle and the seasons may be of more immediate concern to the human Sun-worshipper, whether it be for leisure or survival in growing food. It is this simple yearly pattern which is helpful to observe for meditational purposes.

The present Gregorian calendar almost looks like a subtle device to de-focus your true alignment with the sun's path. The path cannot be changed by human calculations, so the time when the Sun is at its highest (zenith) – the summer solstice – and its lowest – the winter solstice, the spring equinox and autumn equinox (equal night/equal day), form the fixed, quarterly sections of the solar year. These quarters are then divided into cross quarter days, 1 February, 1 May, 1 August and 1 November each year, so we have a rhythm of eight sections to work with the Sun as it appears high in the sky and sinks to its lowest point. These rhythms, marking the changing of the seasons, affect the human mind, body and spirit whether people are aware of it in this way or not.

The cycle of meeting, seeding, birth, nurturing, life, harvesting, decaying and death display this ongoing cycle or circle in the solar year. It should be hardly surprising to find ancient festivals and alignments to sacred points on the ground coinciding with the Sun's path or other planetary bodies and stars. It is one way of bringing an understanding of 'heaven' to Earth.

In a personal way, we can view the Sun as representing the spirit and the Moon as representing the Soul in symbolic, esoteric terms, especially when meditating in our 'inner temples'.

The Moon

It is the cycle of the Moon which can cause confusion when we try to fit it into a solar year, for the moon's motion and its interplay with the Sun and Earth is complex. However, for our purposes, it is enough to find out when the new Moon and full Moon occur each month, for meditating with the moon's phases can bring about an immediate, daily, weekly, monthly effect which can be used to great advantage.

The Moon's effect on the tidal flow of our planet is often used as an example to show how a celestial body can affect the human body. The 75 per cent water content in our bodies responds to the phases of the Moon, bringing about some strange effects in some people, particularly at new and full moons, (loony – lunar). We literally go in and out with the tides wherever we are!

The orbit of the Moon around the Earth takes twenty-nine days, which was called a 'moonth' and we now call a 'month'. Its day of the week is Monday or Moon day. There are four stages of the Moon taking place in a month which we can use to advantage by flowing with the cycle in the following way:

First stage Dark Moon, when it is not visible for four days and then becomes a new Moon. A time of full Earth because the light energies are withdrawn. This is a time for thinking, contemplating and meditating to explore possibilities, create new ideas and make plans. A time of seeking peace within.

Second stage Waxing Moon for eleven days. A fast-flowing growth which is moving towards us. A period when we should work on what needs to be attracted or brought into everyday life. Self motivation is important during this period in starting new projects and launching new ideas and when affirmations are emphasised during meditations.

Third stage Full Moon for three days. The third day is the night of full Moon. Its total influence holds two days prior to full Moon and two days after – a powerful five days for meditating. The Moon receives the total reflection of the Sun. Think of the Moon in your left hand and the Sun in your right hand, with you (the Earth) in the middle when meditating at this time. This is a time of culmination and fulfilment when things should be completed with lots of activity and brought into a state of perfection. Those short-term plans and ideas formulated at new Moon now come into fruition. Long-term plans should have come to a positive stage. A time for meditations on all self-healing sequences, communion with the Higher Self, the angelic and nature kingdoms and prayer, and meditations for peace and planetary healing.

Fourth stage Waning Moon for eleven days. The energies are flowing away – there is an outgoing activity. This is a time for getting rid of things and circumstances that have outlived their purpose as well as giving to others what we have learned or derived from our own efforts and experiences. We can continue to meditate/pray for peace and healing for others and establish suitable affirmations in this connection. A time for giving and learning to receive with grace.

Now we are back to the beginning of the cycle again – the first stage of the dark Moon, which is a resting period, to consider further plans from the experiences recently learned. We can now consider further possibilities in the monthly cycle ahead. To be in harmony with the moon's cycle has the effect of placing us in harmony with the Earth and thus we are synchronising with earth's pulse. To strengthen this connection further, we can match the cycle through our breathing practice just for relaxation or in preparing for meditation.

Exercise 14: Moon Breathing

1   Breathe in to the count of eleven (this matches the new Moon/waxing Moon through eleven days).
2   Hold the breath to the count of three (this matches the three days of full Moon).
3   Breathe out to the count of eleven (this matches the eleven days of waning Moon).
4   Pause (hold) before next inhaling for four counts (this matches four days of dark Moon), continue breathing in to eleven, hold for three, exhale for eleven, pause for four counts. Try to visualise the Moon's phases as you breathe through this exercise.

At first, you may find breathing in for eleven counts is slightly difficult, but you will soon adjust to this pattern, for it will balance both body and mind as you continue. Try at least six sets of this pattern to start with and gradually increase the sequence each day, or to a number which feels comfortable for you.

The element water is associated with the Moon (tides) and with the emotional body or emotions in the human body. We *feel* this energy in waves or in *motion* as it touches the heart and spirit. We can be lost in a sea of emotions as we battle with an emotional crisis.

In order to survive, we need to let go of the attachments of the past – emotional blackmail, 'attitude' or deep habit which has held a sense of security. To adjust to the sense of loss in the midst of deep grief is to try to regain the sense of 'self'. The sense of loss has many deep levels, but however poignant, your survival back into wholeness depends on your regaining your personal power, your Life Force. Get a friend to join you in Moon breathing and re-align your emotional body which will build a sense of peace and acceptance of the 'present'. Emotions need to be surfaced rather than buried. The Angel of Peace will carry you through the breath. You have only to ask.

Cosmic connections

The measurable pulse of Earth and the sounds our own space vehicles have recorded coming from the planetary bodies in our solar system indicate their cosmic vibrations. It is through these that we are all connected, not only to our home planet but to our solar system and the stars beyond.

Pythagoras taught long ago about the 'Music of the Spheres', a concept to be understood on many levels, which is worth further research for the serious seeker. With cosmic connections in mind, let us explore and try to discover a personal concept through a meditation.

Exercise 15: Exploring Inner and Outer Space

Prepare your space and sit comfortably, close your eyes and go through the full procedures of protection, Earth Star/Soul Star (Higher Self) connection and relaxation.

Focus your eyes upon the 'inner screen' (inside your forehead). Visualise your door set in the wall. This time we are visiting our own inner temple, so when you are ready ... open the door and step into the hallway. Close the door behind you. There are steps in front of you leading up into your personal, sacred space – your inner temple. Let it be as beautiful as possible in this very moment. Know that this place is your sanctuary. This is your inner power centre of peace.

Go up the few steps and look for a light burning – this is your Eternal Flame which is never extinguished. Now look for the centre point in this place where there is an unusual, comfortable chair in the middle of a circle. Sit down and relax ... call upon your guardians to be fully present with you. Now visualise a translucent, shimmering pyramid around yourself with the four sides: one in front, one behind and one on each side and joining at the apex above your head. The fifth side is the base or floor. Use your breath to create this five-sided vehicle ... just breathe it around yourself. Relax ... This vehicle can take you safely anywhere you wish to explore. For the purposes of this meditation, it is an observation vehicle to view the solar system.

Clearly request your Higher Self to 'lift-off' and feel the sensation of moving upwards and out into a dark but clear, starry sky. You are heading for the viewing platform of a central space station beyond the Moon. You are quite safe.

Take your time to adjust to the velvety, deep dark blue colour of indigo space.

The first pause on this journey is in the vicinity of the Moon. From here, look back at planet Earth suspended and turning in space – a beautiful, blue-green sphere ... remember what you see and feel ...

Now move up and beyond the Moon until you reach the central control viewing platform. Let your vehicle come gently to rest. Through the vehicle's sides, look down at the whole of the solar system. Take your time to observe the Earth, Sun, Moon, Mercury, Venus, Mars, Jupiter, Saturn, Uranus, Neptune and Pluto. Watch their movements or get an impression of how they move in constant motion, dancing a great cosmic dance together. Remember what you see and feel ... Do you see any colour? Do you hear any sounds? On this first viewing, your focus has to be maintained, so do not linger too long ...

It is time to return. Instruct your Higher Self for a homeward journey and feel your vehicle lift off gently, moving down towards the Moon and Earth ... it only takes seconds. You gently enter down into your temple and the vehicle comes to rest. All is still and tranquil in your temple's peaceful space. Step out of your five-sided pyramid. Thank your guardians and move towards your door. Hanging beside the door is a cloak. Put it on, pulling the hood over your head. Feel it warm and protective as you wrap it around yourself. Open the door and step onto the threshold, closing the door behind you.

You are now closing down, allowing the Higher Self to shift into the correct level for you at this time. You are returning to full consciousness remembering everything you have experienced, bringing back the beauty of the Cosmos into your life. Starting at twelve, place the golden disc with the etched cross upon it to seal each chakra as the number is said (slowly). 12 ... 11 ... 10 ... 9 ... 8 ... 7 ... 6 ... 5 ... 4 ... 3 ... 2 ... 1 ... to the knees, the feet and the Earth Star. Take some deep breaths, move hands and feet ... open your eyes and stretch ... Without speaking, write down all your impressions.

Go to the nearest tap and let cold water trickle over your arms, wrists and hands, and then have something to eat and drink.

Summary

* By now, you will have found that taping the meditations enables you to relax fully and complete the exercises without having to remember the instructions. It keeps you fully in command.

* The experiences cannot be achieved by any other means except through your own consciousness in a state of meditation when exploring inner and outer space.

* You will notice that you are always placed in a safe environment to achieve the higher state of consciousness.

* In this exercise, the vehicle we use for moving the consciousness in outer space – a five-sided pyramid is not only a protection device, but resonates with different dimensional levels – a time-space vehicle. It forms an ancient geometrical pattern compatable to this planet and humanity. There are other, more sophisticated patterns that can be learned.

* Many people use the construct of the inner temple for meditation and once you are comfortable with the preparation exercises, use this as your power centre to meet your Higher Self, your guardians and to receive instruction or answers to your questions.

* Reading through each exercise beforehand obviously helps you to focus – that is the left-hand brain link. If you haven't done anything like this before, you may still find it difficult to keep up the focus on an idea which may seem ridiculous to your ego and subconscious mind. It does take practice and may require some re-programming initially, but these steps in creative meditation lead you to expand your mind safely while having fun.

* Once more, don't force anything. If you can't get on with this idea at present, concentrate on those you can.

* Remember, there really are no limits to what can be achieved eventually and there is no competition with anyone else. The reward of perseverance brings you towards the skill of 'remote viewing' where you project your mind to a given target for observation.

* Integrity and responsibility are always present when new skills are accessed, which means that it is against universal law to interfere or impose one's will upon that of another. That is lower ego stuff. The value we are working for is for the highest possible good for ourselves and others. Sounds high-minded? Yes, of course it is – we are going for gold!

131

11
Meditation guidelines for young people

The generation gap is really a difference in consciousness – the space between people – and not the difference in years

In this chapter we explore a way of finding the Power of Peace for the younger generation in a simple, uncomplicated way through interacting with the Animal kingdom and the Angel Within. The focus is on relaxation, which forms the basis of all kinds of meditation. *The greater the capacity for relaxation, the greater the capacity for action*.

During the earlier years leading up to the teens, many children have experiences of 'seeing' people – perhaps a grandparent or other close relative who had passed on, or an awareness of a shiny, peaceful and loving being (angel?). Other children have clear, out-of-the-body experiences in dreams where they are flying or find they move in an instant without effort. Even nightmares should be observed with much greater interest than is generally held, since many of them are signals that some negative interference is stirring up the energies in the home environment. Children are born with higher sensitivies which gradually recede as the physical and educational training takes over. Most sensitive experiences from young children are accepted by them as being normal and it isn't until they relate them to parents or guardians that they find it is unacceptable to talk about or believe in such 'rubbish'. If the parents were brought up and programmed to cancel such material, it is likely that they would pass on this coding. In the present times, so many children, young and older people are having unusual experiences that soon these will be more 'normal' than not – numbers will outweigh the cynics.

Answers are also coming through at a greater rate from people who are researching ghost stories or other unusual events like crop circles and UFOs. Be wary of the sensational as well as the glib explanations. Nowadays, there is a lot of sensible material available from experienced observers.

The teenage years are a period of curiosity and enquiry into these matters and often, experiments are launched without careful thought or research as to how and why supernatural events occur. The door can sometimes be opened to lower, interfering energies. Horror movies add to negative programming. Meditating can detox the mind and bring fresh focus and insight to all kinds of sensational material.

Because there are so many physical changes and growth patterns going berserk throughout the teenage period, the idea of sitting quietly to adventure into inner landscapes might seem a waste of time to some. They may feel they need to be much more physically active. Tai chi, Chi gong and Yoga are all ways of developing a state of tranquillity while activating the body, which develops disciplined focus, has terrific health benefits and is fun. A state of 'meditation in action' describes these types of activity and they are highly recommended. Good training in the various martial arts available now may suit other temperaments.

There are times when study worries and other stresses threaten to spiral downward into a depressive state and although it may be only temporary, can be extremely disconcerting and fearful. The confused, inner resources may seem lacking if called upon in a crisis. The practice of some form of creative meditational focus builds up the inner resources in a subtle way, through the chemical changes occurring in the body during this quiet state, which strengthens the individual so that mood swings are decreased and a sense of calm can be accessed.

Most people, young and old, are generally operating in a frame of mind which has become used to the idea that everything that happens to us is happening *outside ourselves* or coming at us from outside, or that all the causes are outside ourselves. This presupposes that we are at times helpless and can at any time be the victim of circumstance. We are the observers, constantly on the look-out for danger. We are taught to survive from all the possible dangers lurking 'out there'. We have been programmed to fear. In being in this state even subconsciously, we are lowering our natural Life Force and the power of fear controls just about everything we do. When this state gets too intense, the stress factor in our bodies moves to overload. Fear needs to be recognised as an insidious force which need not be challenged head-on but replaced with skills to build confidence and the recognition of inner resources which are secure and loving.

Remember what was said in an earlier chapter – *Upon that which you place attention, so power is given to it.*

Such is the power of fear. It is only a threat to us personally, if we allow it to be. The popular phrase 'False Evidence Appearing Real' is a good description of fear being created with 'What if ... such and such happens?' It *won't* happen, unless you give it a strong fear thought-form of power.

In all the preceding chapters, we have built an understanding as to who and what we really are. Meditation guidelines have been suggested as to how to reclaim our natural energies and motivate ourselves into action for self-healing, relaxation or spiritual endeavour through finding the Power of Peace. While we are learning and partaking in this development, fear is gradually dispelled. Optimism takes over.

The Animal kingdom

The Animal kingdom on this planet is now working on a global scale to help us re-programme ourselves through the power of love and compassion. They are in service as companions, healers and teachers with no conditions attached. Many of the species are leaving the planet. Like all the kingdoms of this planet, there is a duality operating here, where portions of species operate with the lower energies and are not equipped as yet to be of the same service as others. Everything has its place in each kingdom, both in location on the planet and in interaction with each other for mutual benefit. A great deal of information about the family of cetaceans (dolphins, whales and porpoises) has been accessed in the last few years because the consciousness of the human race has identified more closely with the Animal kingdom in general than at any other time in modern history. (We'll have a closer look at them later.)

The concern of humans for animal welfare has opened up many other areas of activity between the two during the last years of the twentieth century. Among them are horse whispering, animal healing, observing whales and swimming with dolphins. The close contact we establish with domestic pets teaches the ability of communication without words on the physical plane – telepathy. The story of Dr Dolittle and recent movies about 'talking' animals has brought the Animal kingdom into focus.

People with a great feeling for creatures of the Animal kingdom have always found the animals 'talking' to them where they were able to communicate about their pains and other feelings. This isn't something new – it's just that these activities are highlighted in the public arena nowadays so more people are informed.

Most people in the past had become conditioned to treat animals as having inferior intelligence, not realising they should sometimes just listen to them. The people who didn't like to say too much about what they knew in the past for fear of ridicule (but did it anyway) are the ones who silently opened doors for humanity to feel its compassion for the Animal kingdom. The healing of animals through accepted ways plus holistic methods is now widespread.

The next step is to realise that our pets are in a constant healing mode for us, and will process large quantities of negative energy in and around the domestic environment. Cats will curl up beside you if you are ill or seek your lap, and they aren't just happy with the extra warmth – they are healing you – processing your negative energies. In so doing, many of them can take on too much and as a result, become ill themselves.

Dolphins and whales

It has been established and proven widely that dolphins are great healers. They have a Soul connection with humans and are our guardians, for they easily sense and understand the human energy field, but their telepathic capacity is way beyond human ability, for it is multi-dimensional. (Their consciousness capacity is at least equal to fifth-dimensional.)

The sensing, sonic abilities they share with whales and porpoises serve not only their own survival needs, but ours too, in keeping a balance in the waters of the oceans. When they salute humans by leaping and playing, they display freedom and joy which they are endeavouring to convey to us. They are doing all they can to raise our awareness in these times of great change. Laughter, joy and play have a high energy frequency which disperses low, dark frequencies.

If you aren't fortunate enough to have experienced dolphins physically, you can call upon them in creative meditation or ask for dream contact so you may learn from them.

This may sound at first like fantasy, but after all – humans are deeply moved by stories made into movies and are therefore touched by the energy – and movies are created illusion with a message. You can make your own inner film through visualisation and access the telepathic streams which connect you to a real, physical dolphin. If you have swum with a dolphin or watched a display by them, you may like to use a particular name you heard to make your connection during the following visualisation sequence. If not, you can ask your dolphin for its name when you are playing with it in the sequence. Dolphins are now known as the Record Keepers of the planet, for they have kept and stored the history of the Earth in their memories. Their energy comes from the heart, and because of their ability and mission to respond to humans, are always ready to receive your wavelength, wherever you live in the world. There are two exercises coming up: the first is a dolphin exercise. Use it for visualisation just before you go to sleep to promote peaceful *dreaming*. The second is for re-charging yourself with the breath, to give peace and balance through *relaxation*.

1   The preparation is minimal in the case of the 'sleep for dreaming' sequence. Once you're ready for bed you're ready to dream – except – always having a small notebook beside your bed so that the following morning you can record any dreams that occurred. This could come in the form of an answer to any question you asked or something that was helpful that was conveyed to you.

Dreaming with dolphins is protected as all occurs in a higher dimension.

2   For relaxation: this doesn't mean relaxing and then sliding off into sleep! This is good for programming your mind into concentrated awareness that will gradually build into gaining more focus upon any activity.

It is a stressbuster to relax the body so that the focus is keeping the mind alert (handy for exams or public speaking).

Exercise 16: Dream Swimming with Your Dolphin

(Non-swimmers should not be put off – the waters we encounter in the dream are super-safe and you are able to breathe underwater in the same way as you breathe now. The conditions are very special and very different from our third-dimensional world. Here, you only have to think what you want to do – and you do it.)

On the first occasion you try this, just go for the experience and get used to the idea. You should be almost ready for sleep, warm and relaxed, lying comfortably in your bed. Make sure you have your notebook and pen ready for the morning. if you don't remember anything when you wake up, then say so in your journal entry – and the date. Later on, when you are used to dolphin dreaming and have asked a question or two or have something to record, you will be glad you were prepared, especially when you read through your notes in a month or two. You are likely to see a story or pattern emerging. We have to remember that in only a few moments on waking, dreams can disappear and be forgotten.

To enter into the sequence, imagine a door in front of you, set in a wall. This is your door, your way into the inner spaces. Know that as you enter you are protected. Examine the door and remember its colour and shape. See the door handle. Grasp and turn it and go through, closing the door behind you. You are on a path which leads to a beach. This is your very own, private beach. The sun is shining in a cloudless blue sky. Move onto the beach and feel the soft, warm sand under your feet and the gentle warmth of the sun on your body. The waves are gently lapping over the soft, golden sand. The water is pure and clear. Paddle in the water and feel it warm and pleasant as you scan the blue sea. Call for your dolphin to come and play. Imagine a beam coming from your forehead sending out this message. Watch and wait for the dolphin to leap above the waters and salute you. When you see it, you can dive into the water and meet.

The dolphin will always talk to you in your own language and you will just know how to communicate. Follow it under the water where you will be able to breathe quite normally for this is a sacred place. Relax in the warmth of the water and let the dolphin nudge you and invite you to hold on to it so you can skim through the waves together. Remember how it feels. Now ask the dolphin to stay with you in your sleep and relax and float in the warm water, letting it gently rock you, safely and gently.

As you relax, let go of all your worries and any stress of the past. Let the Power of Peace in the waters wash through you and heal any aches or pains. See everything washed away and dissolve in the water.

Now, if you wish, you can move onto the beach where you become instantly dry and you can stretch out on the soft sand and lie in the warm sunshine quite safely. Your dolphin is close by and in contact. Relax, more and more, feeling calm and at peace, letting the energy of the sand softly support you as you drift deeper and deeper into sleep ... all is well ... you will awaken in the morning relaxed and refreshed, recalling all that you need to remember that is right for you at this time.

137

Exercise17: Relaxation Worth an Hour of Sleep

Allow about ten to fifteen minutes minimum. There are two short parts to this and they can be done separately or together as a sequence. Try them first together.

Stretch out comfortably on your bed with shoes off and remove any clothing that feels restricting. Place a cover over you if it is cold. Make sure no one will disturb you. Realise that the bed is supporting you and will do all the work in taking your weight.

a   As you lie on your back, place your right hand upon your right shoulder and as you breathe in, slowly lift the right elbow up as high as you can – stretch it. Feel the shoulder muscles responding and the waist stretching. Don't strain with these movements and don't do this quickly, but lift slowly on the breath in, hold the breath to the count of three and bring the elbow down on the exhale of the breath. Repeat with the left hand on the left shoulder, breathing in and lifting the left elbow up as high as possible. Hold the breath for three counts and lower the elbow as you breathe out. Continue for a minimum of six slow movements for each elbow, alternating between right and left. Rest. (This exercise will ease shoulder and back tension).

b   Now place one hand on your lower abdomen and breathe normally. Focus on your hand and observe what is happening as you breathe in your normal way.

As you calmly breathe in and out, watch for changes in where and how the breath is moving. Gradually, the lift in the abdomen gets lower and lower. Observe the pause between breaths. Keep your attention on the hand and the breath until the lift in the lower abdomen is underneath your hand. Let the breath wash through your body into every cell. This is a Breath of Peace. Keep it going but do not actually go to sleep. Enjoy the feeling of being completely calm and relaxed. Say to yourself: 'I am calm and relaxed and I am not drifting into sleep'.

This is the feeling to reach and hold for meditation which in the previous chapters we attained in the seated, upright position. It needs practice. The rest that you give the body in this way, either lying down or seated, is worth an hour of ordinary sleep. You are re-charging your batteries (your etheric body).

Once you have mastered moving into this abdomen breathing, lying down, without going to sleep, you may like to sit in a comfortable chair and try the abdomen breathing in a seated position to become equally calm and relaxed for energy boosting and as a practice for meditation.

Seeking the Angel Within

Everyone has an inner angel or a self which is operating on a finer frequency and who is always with us, whether we know about it or not.

In previous chapters we have identified this as the Higher Self. It doesn't matter what we call it, it still means the same. This meaning is that everyone carries their own wise, guardian energy within to assist them throughout life. It is the spark of divine force which is always working towards your higher interests. Some people call it 'God-force'. It is highly protective and discriminating, working as part of your Soul-force to watch over your earthly experiences operating with the universal laws of non-interference. This means your free will is just that – free.

It is a person's choice whether they wish to evolve through the lessons that are learned through life on this third-dimensional planet or resist and thus keep repeating the same type of event or circumstance.

Without getting too complicated, if you have difficult decisions to make where you cannot see a clear answer, then by asking your Angel Within you are tuning in to a frequency which is not only clearer but holds the blueprint about your mission on Earth.

This is serious fun and not to be treated in any way as spooky. That ploy is promoting fear which lowers your energy field. How can you be afraid of yourself? Your Angel Within will not give you the winning answers to competitions and such-like, but will assist with difficulties and tests you encounter if you are sincere with your requests. All it requires is respect for this higher frequency of yourself where a greater wisdom is operating. Just as we can practice relaxation and flow with the dolphin energies, so the Angel Within will inspire you with the best advice and act as a gatekeeper to guard you from unhelpful vibes. It is doing this anyway, but it becomes more apparent when you decide to ask. There are other angelic beings, or they can be called angelic frequencies (or energies), whose job is to respond to our requests for assistance or protection, as outlined in Chapter 6.

Making contact with your Angel Within is achieved by *merely thinking of it*, wherever you may be, but consciously to feel the presence needs a little more effort and practice.

139

Exercise18: Feel the Angel Within

1   To enter into this sequence, relax into a comfortable chair and make sure you will not be disturbed.

2   Always make sure your legs are uncrossed with both feet firmly on the ground. Close your eyes.

3   Before you start, mentally request your Angel Within to surround you with the Power of Peace and Protection. Imagine a shield of white light energy around you.

4   Listen to your breathing and with one hand on your abdomen, continue to breathe until the breath moves your abdomen underneath your hand. Feel the breath as if it is washing through you, relaxing every muscle and bone in your body. Take your time.

5   When you are ready, move your hand from the abdomen and place it on your *heart area* and try to complete the following simple visualisation by focusing your inner attention as if to the inside of your forehead.

Imagine a door in front of you, set in a wall. This is your door, your way into the inner spaces. Remember its colour and shape. Grasp and turn the door handle and open the door. Go through, closing the door behind you. You are in a beautiful courtyard with a fountain of water in the centre. The water sparkles in the sunshine as it rises up and falls down into the surrounding pool. Listen to the sound it makes ... There is a seat with soft cushions nearby. Sit down and watch the fountain playing. You hear the sound of the water and see the rainbow colours in the spray. Everything around you is calm, warm and peaceful. Ask your Angel Within to become more present in the hand touching your heart. Wait and focus on your hand and heart area for some moments (long pause ... keep up the focus and feel any changes). You will remember all that you experience. You will remember this meeting place. You can return at any time.

When you are ready, move towards the door, open it and step through, closing it behind you. Ask the Angel Within to surround you with protection as you take some deep breaths and pull all your energies around yourself and to your solar plexus and heart areas. Imagine a door closes here, which acts like a shield. Take a deep breath and slowly start to move your hands and feet and stretch your arms. Open your eyes. When you are ready, go immediatly and wash your hands. Let the cold water trickle over your wrists. Then make any notes which will record your feelings and observations (with the date). It is important to eat and drink something now which will ground all your energies.

Do not attempt to introduce anything more into the visualization with your imagination until you feel confident about the contact, for it is designed to keep you focused on the aim. It is so easy to become distracted and thus forget your original intent.

Practise this sequence about once a week to start with and when you have practised it many times over and read your notes, you will know much more about this gentle way of contact and you will have trained your mind to respond to your commands, rather than the mind waffling about all over the place with random thoughts.

Your confidence, concentration and inspiration will increase and strengthen. You can put your hand on your heart as a signal to the Angel Within at any time, anywhere, whenever you need it.

12

Health, wealth and happiness, and the value of peace

If you were to be granted just one wish for your lifetime out of health, wealth or happiness, which would you choose?

This was the question posed in the first chapter. What did you choose and have you changed your mind after reading or experiencing the suggestions for meditation in the chapters that followed?

Initially, of course, we would like to have all three; but have you concluded that now there is one which forms a basis for relieving your troubles in this present moment?

Whatever your choice, the question of what you *value* most in life, your investment in it, your rate of exchange with others and the rewards or expectations which result, are all hidden in the choice of either health, wealth or happiness.

Through the ability to meditate, decision-making is made easier.

Contemplation, prayer, pondering, worrying over facts and figures are ways of thinking we employ in decision-making but meditation takes you into steps beyond the intellectual. As we have experienced in the exercises, it gives added ingredients – space, detachment and peace where perceptions are lifted. In that peaceful place, inspiration can flower. A free perspective is gained when you are in a state of timeless observation and in tune with the Infinite. The answer unfolds.

Looking at the world in a totally *physical* way, without regard or knowledge of this greater picture, is limiting to the extent that every question has to be answered with only a physical, 3D solution. There are no *real* alternatives to a materialistic, closed point of view, because it is a fixed, repetitive pattern. Let's remind ourselves by looking back at health, wealth and happiness in this old way.

Health

We are born with the ability to heal ourselves – we cut ourselves and the wound heals. We are taught how to feed, wash and care for our body in our early years. Through illness, we discover that the body can feel as if it's falling to pieces. When health is regained, we are relieved and then we tend to take it for granted. As we get older, a fear of ill-health is often prominent in our minds. By this time, we have forgotten how well the body can heal itself, because we lost contact with its real needs in the hurly-burly of life. We also had a good shot at poisoning it with a variety of concoctions. Some of these we didn't even know were there (nobody told us). If somebody tried, we didn't believe them at the time. The body just got more and more tired of trying to heal itself. However, some of us decided to give our bodies more of our attention with exercise, revised eating habits and careful medication, and some just handed their bodies over to an 'authority' when it started to malfunction.

Some people are born with bodily disfunctions and most people discover some along the way. No wonder we might choose unfailing health for the physical body as the wish to be granted for a lifetime. (It is the only one of the three which *describes* Life Force.)

Wealth

Monetary wealth – if only. This would solve all the problems of caring for ourselves and others in this present world. It would buy health care too. We could live in style and luxury, we could travel the world, we could buy ourselves into any experience that took our fancy (provided we had our health). Of course, to manage the wealth, we would have to engage financial experts, and to manage the houses, yachts and cars we will need staff. It is a bit of a responsibility, this financial wheeler-dealing to keep it all secure and flowing to ensure monetary security; and then we may need to put in place security measures for all the property and contents we have acquired.

Perhaps your idea of wealth as the wish for this lifetime is different. Whatever the case, it is something requiring stewardship in a money-orientated society. (Money has no energy of itself. It requires massive inputs of energy to make it work.)

Happiness

If this was your wish – to be in a state of happiness throughout your lifetime, how do you see it working? Happiness is rather difficult to describe – you either are or you aren't. Your awareness of being happy usually hinges upon another person – if they are all right, then you are. If they love you, then you can love them and feel happy – a kind of barter system operating to keep happiness afloat. Happiness comes because you succeeded at something, enjoyed something or someone's company. It is therefore a state usually brought about by or because of something else.

There are some, maybe only a few people, however, who are contented, who always look happy and yet seem to have very little else in terms of wealth or even health. They have *peace of mind*. They have probably succeeded in finding the peace within themselves or are in the process of achieving it. They are displaying the state of contentment and joy which everyone has deep within, but few seem to find. Is this what you perceive as happiness for yourself for this lifetime, or does your idea of happiness involve another person? Tricky, isn't it?

Happiness is a state arrived at through the successful application of energy to or for a purpose. It then becomes an energy in itself for a short time, but to last, it needs re-fuelling. To wish for happiness as a constant physical state to be in for this lifetime might be inter-esting or boring. It depends on how it is applied, I suppose, for it could make others happy or it could irritate them to see you so happy. Presumably, to wish for happiness means one would be happy under all circumstances – in a state of harmony.

The greater picture
To look at health, wealth and happiness from other viewpoints than the purely physical is to take into account all that we have been exploring in this book and to consider how you now feel about them all from *your* point of view.

What did you write in the cover of this book at the start? Have your values changed in any way? Have you, or are you going to make more of an investment in yourself by changing any attitudes regarding your health? Are you committed yet to meditating regu-larly – perhaps for a 'wealth' of health or a 'wealth' of happiness (harmony)?

For greater health, the information in Chapter 2 revealed that *all* the parts that make up the whole will require attention when a 'dis-ease' finally manifests at the end of the line – in *the physical body*.

Maintaining health, not only in body but in mind and spirit, will allow the Life Force to flow freely into all areas of existence. The 3D spacesuit *needs* responsible maintenance to all its parts.

Your wealth in the greater picture has to do with values, appreciation and how abundance is perceived beyond the material. It covers personal attributes and skills and being aware of the beauty in all things. We speak of having a 'wealth' of experience. The value in our meditations, where there are experiences on the inner planes which are often awesome, may also be understood as being 'beyond price'. Of course, there are many more examples of 'wealth' perceptions.

On the monetary level, learning the skills of finance is a drama of profit and loss which gives the Soul many valuable lessons. This may be the Soul mission in this lifetime: to balance the knowledge and experience of wealth.

Having a wealthy, personal magnetism is the result of gaining an ability to respond in the right way from an all-round, higher viewpoint which in itself magnetises all that you need at exactly the right time.

Is happiness in the greater picture a result of peace of mind, body and spirit? The word 'happiness' is a perception – a limiting belief. We also have to be careful about using the word contentment, since a contented state can be a place of satisfaction and conclusion which prevents the discovery of anything new. The continuity, the movement and dance of life brings changes. To be in harmony, to bring all that you are into a healthy, resonating, energy field and to flow with awareness is treasure of the spirit – it is operating with *joy*.

The simple scenario describing the art class in Chapter 1 was really demonstrating *many* levels of understanding and observation.

While all the points of view from the twelve observers in the art class contributed their individual, angular views around the circle, their *collective* description made up the group's *whole, all-round view* of the subject. You can see that *the success of the whole depends solely on the quality of input by the parts,* or, what the individual achieves (or doesn't) *affects the whole*. Taking this one step further, think of humanity in the world as a whole, with all its varied parts: wonderful races, cultures, traditions and beliefs etc.

The input of humanity living day to day, year by year and generation through generation, results in a collective consciousness which is added to as humanity evolves and forms a record of its evolution. (This record is established on the etheric plane.)

Each single part, each single human, is a cog in the wheel of this collective memory bringing their race, beliefs and structure to bear on each present moment. The past has brought us to this 'now'. Looking at the sum total of this 'now' from humanity's point of view we can see that all the past dramas on the world stage with which we are most uncomfortable are now really surfacing to be dealt with and harmonised. This is the mark of entry into a new age – the Age of Aquarius, known as the Age of the Brotherhood of Man.

It is a timely opportunity to recognise that if the individual parts of the whole healed and harmonised themselves, this input would bring about collective humanity's transformation. Impossible? Only if the past is dwelt upon in a negative way and hope is buried with a doom and gloom scenario. Prophecy is not about what *is* going to happen – it's about what *could* happen as viewed from the present moment. Tomorrow's prophecy could be different because of some unexpected input. Any intervention holding critical mass can rearrange things to affect that prophetic future – in the twinkling of an eye. Prophecy is an advance warning. Unfulfilled prophecy is successful prophecy.

Can one person really make a difference?

All over the world, there are many groups from *all* traditions and races who are meditating and working at bringing about a balance to redress the world's negativity. This may seem an impossible task, but they maintain constant, creative, peaceful, healing thoughts which form a light that is so strong that it can consume and transform negativity immediately.

This action is *only* successful when carried out with no hidden agendas, without conditions, (unconditional love for all human dilemmas) and for the Highest Possible Good, (the best possible scenario according to Divine Law).

Think of thousands and thousands of groups and individuals regularly meditating on thoughts of healing, harmony, love, light and peace for humanity and the planet. You can imagine this great thought-form building into a critical mass of human endeavour. Positive action for the greater good means action *without judgment* – not choosing who or where on the globe needs the focus, but just putting individual quality into the 'collective' bank and leaving distribution to the natural law of flow through the Greatest/Highest Source of Goodness in the Universe, which ensures the best possible scenario for any drama or horror playing itself out on Earth.

There is no agency that can *initiate* this silent service other than humanity itself, because the free will of humanity is sacred in universal law. Just one more person adding to the *collective goodwill* for the Power of Peace, *can* make all the difference. The charitable, loving, practical work and support on the ground for those who are desperate is another expression which many want and need to be involved with but if the thought-forms of peace and harmony are quietly upheld too, only then are we truly building balance into the future on a planetary scale, while patching up the emergencies of life.

To accomplish the *highest* levels of mind, body and spirit understanding – to see the view from every angle and to be aware of a greater picture no matter what the subject, is only achieved by shifting your level of consciousness little by little, to become integrated with your Higher Self and your total Life-force (or God-force) and bring it into daily life.

Good intent and persistence have immense value and humanity is making great headway in developing the loving compassion of the heart.

As we have found, meditation develops mind expansion and if this practice, together with positive thinking in daily life, is pursued *no matter what is going on in the outer world*, then the Soul gains more love and wisdom to achieve its highest goals. Success is consequently enhanced in all of life's endeavours and the individual affects all others around them. Again, this is how one person can really make the difference. It is very simple. It starts with one, develops into the many which becomes the whole.

When we apply the greater picture to looking at our subjects of health, wealth and happiness, we can maybe see that they are really not separated one from another. They are inter-related. By using them together, we can bring to bear all aspects and meanings on many levels.

For example, we can once more use affirmations during meditation to build the ideas into strong, positive thought-forms which re-programme formerly held, negative attitudes. Here are some examples:

Affirmation for health

✳ Every cell of my physical body radiates with health.
✳ All my subtle bodies and chakras radiate with health.
✳ My mind is filled with healthy and vibrant thoughts and I feed my Soul with divine health through my loving Higher Self.
✳ I am building a healthy body, mind and spirit which radiates a healthy abundance into all areas of my life.

(These areas mean your bank balance, relationships, work, hobbies etc.)

Affirmation for health, wealth and happiness

✳ An abundance of health, wealth and happiness pervades every cell of my body.
✳ I am filled with vibrant health, wealth and happiness in every atom, molecule and cell of my being which radiates joy and abundance into all areas of my life.

Repeat the affirmations three times and visualise a white light of abundance flowing into every cell.

These are very powerful, creative thought-forms which need your sincere intent behind them so that they can be built into your life structure and have maximum effect. Like attracts like so that if you are half-hearted about this – or anything else for that matter – then the results will speak for themselves. Above all, be patient. Results may take a while to manifest although you should start to feel really good after a few days.

Meditation is at the root – the basis of all other mind expansion skills.

There are many valuable meditation disciplines taught throughout the world which suit different races, cultures and belief systems and there is no competition as to which is best. Each is a route to self-discovery and it has so often been said that there are many paths to the top of the mountain. Whatever the chosen path, everyone can benefit in their own individual way. What is right for you, is not necessarily right for others.

Using the creative meditation exercises has enabled us to touch on moving the consciousness for remote viewing which we used for the observation of the solar system but can be used for any chosen location or target.

You can also explore possible past and future lives, but there are many steps to negotiate before acquiring reasonable skill with these ideas; and some people are not always suited to such expansion for it can use a great deal of physical and mental energy plus, dedication and reasonable health are necessary. Teachers will facilitate the journey and should be sought if you feel inclined towards developing these skills. Ask your Higher Self for assistance.

Some people are born with a natural psychic gift. This needs training and development if it is to be used for the person's best interests and those whom they serve. (In the same way, a very gifted child will develop to the height of their special ability with good teaching, training and practice.)

There is a wide range of natural, psychic ability in humanity and to identify what is going on in the world at the present time regarding its use can be simplified by stating that there are basically two forms of psychism – the higher and the lower – which appeal to either the higher or the lower nature in humankind.

The higher guidance comes from the Higher Self, Soul and higher spiritual planes.

The lower guidance comes from the sub-conscious and the astral or emotional plane where there is distorted or lower quality information.

When people channel information from spiritual sources, it is wise to find out from which level they are operating. Higher sources information will be channelled through either the heart, throat and crown chakras, or all three in unison. Intelligence and wisdom are apparent. It will come in the form of guidelines, creative information and encouragement, and it will always honour everyone's free will with no conflict of religious interests. Love and inspiration are always felt which empowers the receiver. Information conveyed will be for the good of humanity/society/ and will be relevant to assist the present progress of everyone concerned.

Lower sources information is channelled through the solar plexus area – the emotional centre. Channelled information can be conflicting in some way for its connections are to the world of emotion and illusion where the aim is to satisfy curiosity, create glamour and flatter lower egos. Fear, spookiness, mystery, negativity, power-seeking, demands for attention (lower entities) and claims for being an authority are all connected to the contact of lower streams of activity.

Discernment is one of the primary lessons to be learned. This means remaining alert to seek the highest quality from your own inner guidance and always go to the ultimate Source for divine truth. There is a feeling of 'rightness', joy and enthusiasm about truth and it can be found and felt in the *heart*.

The value of Peace

The Power of Peace is infinite. It has infinite depth and infinite levels to be discovered and unfolded from within each person in meditation. Peace has to be experienced first in order to understand just what it means and this understanding is only limited by the quality of the experience, yet every unfolding you achieve has its own beautiful essence leading to the next ... and the next. The Power of Peace is present within *everything* and on *every level*. In meditation it is most apparent when you come to the point of communion with – let us call it – All There Is, the Great Silence or the Great Peace. This is the place *between* thoughts where there is eternal harmony. When this pattern is extended gradually with practice by listening to the Great Silence and holding that place of harmony within, then all thought is suspended. You have extended 'the place between' and are experiencing the eternal state of harmony – that is the Power of Peace, resting in the true essence of Universal Love. This is the only *permanent* state of being, where you are all-knowing, for the little personality ego is set aside and you are in your true 'I am' presence. You have embraced Golden Infinity.

In the previous chapters, the meditation exercises have a point within them where it is suggested that you 'sit and breathe in the atmosphere', 'seek the stillness and let it wash over you' or similar suggestions where you hold the pattern of tranquillity for a few minutes. This is the point or peak to which you have been led by visualisation and into which you can plunge and experience the Great Peace. Whatever depth you experience, you will then bring it back to daily life, because *you* have unfolded it within *yourself*.

In the outer world, if we interviewed a random selection of folk on the High Street asking them what is the opposite to peace ... most would reply ... war. Or if we asked, 'What is peace?' the reply is usually, 'The absence of war'. This is a programming from the human experiences of survival against conflicts over hundreds and hundreds of years in the past and to the present times. It is understandable. War games have been a priority in the human experience.

If we ask what does world peace mean, again the reply may be that there are no nations or factions in any part of the world who are at war or in conflict. A great, spiritual Master said that peace is possible on a planetary scale only when the individual is able to freely hold peace in the heart (which has not been enforced by political methods or other means).

It will happen because individuals have taken responsibility to open up the layers within themselves so that more and more peace is revealed. As this is accomplished, little by little, the consciousness is raised. When the consciousness is raised in humanity, it describes a maturing process which goes beyond the need to express anger and aggression.

The Age of the Brotherhood of Man

We are already well into the change-over period when brave, spiritual warriors have moved forward and are developing their awareness and in contrast there are others who haven't a clue as to what is really happening. Everyone's time frame varies but resistance to change has been obvious. Change-overs bring conflicts in the outer world to the surface.

At this point, it would seem that all the prayers and meditations for peace are not working. They are. The anger and conflict are surfacing and a great deal comes from deep down and from long ago. It has to surface to be healed and forgiven by anyone who has decided to work in spiritual world service. Not only is this surfacing happening on a planetary scale, but it is happening in each individual's personal life.

Regular meditation and chakra self-healing, as we have shown, is very helpful for personal healing and self maintenance. These times, or End Times as they are called, are different from anything previously experienced by the human psyche.

We are in new territory and must create and adapt to new models. Take heart. Nelson Mandela, in his inaugural speech in 1994, said:

'And as we let our lights shine, we unconsciously give other people permission to do the same.

'As we are liberated from our own fear, our presence automatically liberates others.'

Exercise 19: Rose of Peace Meditation

Prepare your meditation space and then prepare yourself as usual with relaxation, breathing and protection. (You may like to place a fresh rose (any colour) beside your candle, as a symbol of your intent).

Outside noises will not disturb you.

In front of you is your door. Grasp the door handle and open it. Move over the threshold and close the door behind you.

In front of you are the steps leading up to your inner temple. Ascend them and enter into your inner power centre of peace. You can see your Eternal Flame burning. There are flowers everywhere. Choose a rose in bud and holding it in your hand, sit down on the comfortable chair which is set within the circle. Relax. Visualise this rose bud on your 'inner screen' and hold the image there. This is the Rose of Peace. Look at the details of the bud closely.

See the green sepals surrounding the bud begin to move and open slowly. The petals begin to reveal themselves as one by one they open. See the colour and the delicate veins in the petals. All is moving in slow motion ... watch a petal unfurl ... see how it grows from the centre ... smell the fragrance as it opens up and breathe in this peaceful perfume ... Let your breath take the scent deep into your heart with every inbreath ... *feel the heart becoming the rose and the rose becoming your heart* as each petal unfolds ... (You can still see the image of the rose on your inner screen, but you can also feel it in your heart.)

Feel the peace held in the centre of the rose gradually coming to light as it opens up ... let the delicate wave upon wave of peace enfold you and fill your heart as you breathe with each wave ... (long pause).

When the rose is opened, focus into its very centre and move right into it ... into the centre of the Power of Peace ... Rest there letting the soft petals of the rose cradle you in loving peace... Your heartbeat is in perfect rhythm with the pulse of peace ... your breath is in perfect harmony with the pulse of peace... Just let this image wash over your body and take you where it will ... keep in a state of observation ... *do not go to sleep* (long pause...)

It is time to return and your task is to bring back this essence of peace, holding it in your heart. The image of the Rose of Peace is in your heart. Remember all that you have experienced.

Be aware of being in your inner temple. Rise from the chair and return to your door where a dark cloak is hanging beside it. Wrap it warmly around yourself, pulling the hood over your head.

Open the door, pass over the threshold and close it behind you. You are now closing down. Ask the Higher Self to shift back into the present correct level for you at this time. Know you are holding the Power of Peace essence within your heart and returning to full consciousness.

Place the golden disc, the seal, on each chakra as the number is said (slowly) ... 12 ... 11 ... 10 ... 9 ... 8 ... 7 ... 6 ... 5 ... 4 ... 3 ... 2 ... 1 ... to the knees, feet and Earth Star rooting you into the ground. Take some deep breaths ... Move your hands and feet ... open your eyes and stretch ...

Silently thank your guardians and Higher Self for their contact and assistance.

Without speaking, write down and draw if necessary all your impressions.

Have something to eat and drink and wash your hands as usual to ground all your energies properly.

Summary

The idea behind this meditation is to bring you ultimately into more of the Great Peace, the Great Silence. The task is to *desire* to return to daily life with it held in your heart. Every journey adds to your experience and thus adds to your personal fulfilment and transformation. No effort is wasted. You will see your outer world in a different light, for you are 'stepping up' your perceptions of it, and your compassion for the human dilemma will grow. This is not 'heavy' stuff. It is 'light' stuff. It is 'light-hearted' and you will find a lot of humour in your discoveries.

The Power of Peace is held in the essence of the threefold flame of Love, Wisdom and Power where there is greatest Joy.

To assist you in daily life, bring that image into everything you are and everything you do for in that image is your greatest teacher, greatest love ... and permanence.

May you always walk in the Power of Peace.

Further reading

Cooper, J.C., *An Illustrated Encyclopaedia of Traditional Symbols,* Thames & Hudson, 1978

Goodman, Jonathan, *Healing Sounds*, Element Books, 1992

Meadows, Kenneth, *Shamanic Experience,* Earth Quest series, Element Books ,1991

Myss, Caroline, *Anatomy of the Spirit*, Bantam Books, 1997

Rudyar, Dane, *The Galactic Dimension of Astrology*, ASI Publishers, New York, 1975

Schlemmer, Phyllis V. and Jenkins, Palden (compilers), *The Only Planet of Choice*, Gateway Books,1993

Wilde, Stuart, *Affirmations*, White Dove International, Inc.,USA

Reference List of Meditation Exercises, 'Rules' and Procedures

Summary of Full Meditation Procedure

Index